GW00870718

illustrated by
Tracy Staskevich

Jenni Trent Hughes

The Greatest
Relationship
& Dating
Tips in the World

A 'The Greatest in the World' book

www.thegreatestintheworld.com

Illustrations:
Tracy Staskevich

Typesetting:
BR Typesetting

Cover images:
© Iofoto; © Anette Linnea Rasmussen; © Andres Rodriguez; © Lisa F Young
all courtesy of www.fotolia.com

Copy editor:
Bronwyn Robertson
www.theartsva.com

Series creator/editor:
Steve Brookes

Published in 2008 by
The Greatest in the World Ltd, PO Box 3182,
Stratford-upon-Avon, Warwickshire CV37 7XW

Text and Illustrations Copyright © 2008 – The Greatest in the World Ltd.

A CIP catalogue record for this book is available from the British Library
ISBN 978-1-905151-35-6

Printed and bound in China by 1010 Printing International Ltd.

This book is dedicated to anyone out there
who has ever felt either the joy or the pain
that love can bring – hopefully it will bring
you more of the former and less of the latter.

This book would not have been possible
without help from some very important people.

My son Jack for peanut butter and jam
sandwiches in bed. His father Brendan for
spiriting him away so I could write.
Marky Mark – well for being Marky Mark!
Julia, Julie, Steve and Anne for believing in me.
Kaye for keeping me sane.
All the lovely people who come up to me on the
street to share their stories – we are all as one.
But most of all thanks to Ray
for teaching me how to feel safe again.

Contents

A few words from Jenni …

'Love makes the word go round' or so sayeth the songs. From the moment we can walk and talk we are introduced to the concept of Love with a capital 'L'. No sooner has it been established that 'Mummy and Daddy love you' than you are catapulted into the world of fairytales and nursery rhymes. From Adam and Eve, to Cinderella and Prince Charming; Mickey and Minnie, to Shrek and Fiona. Love stories surround us on billboards, in telly adverts, magazines – there is nowhere we can turn to avoid being bombarded with the idea that 'love is all you need'.

Before we start on our journey through the ins-and-outs of Love (with a capital L) I'd like you to define for yourself exactly what you think Love is; and exactly what you think Love isn't. Clarifying your thoughts at the beginning will be invaluable in this process. It will do a lot towards helping you understand your past behaviours. It will help show you where you've gone 'right'. It will probably show where and how you might have made some less than effective choices that ended you up in some less than comfortable situations.

For me, love is not a space you can occupy on your own. You can lust after someone, want to get to know them better, have strong feelings for them; but it is nigh unto impossible to be in love on your own. What I am hoping to accomplish with this book is to give you a wise auntie at your fingertips. Practical no-nonsense advice on all the different aspects of meeting people, starting relationships and nurturing them.

Sometimes with the best will in the world it might go wrong, so there's advice on how to extricate yourself incurring as little damage as possible. Starting over? How do you find the strength? Where do you begin?

Hopefully in this book you will find a lifetime of answers. Good luck!

Jenni x

Dating is like going on a job interview. You don't know if you'll get the job, but if you do well, you get to see the interviewer naked.

Anon

Finding love

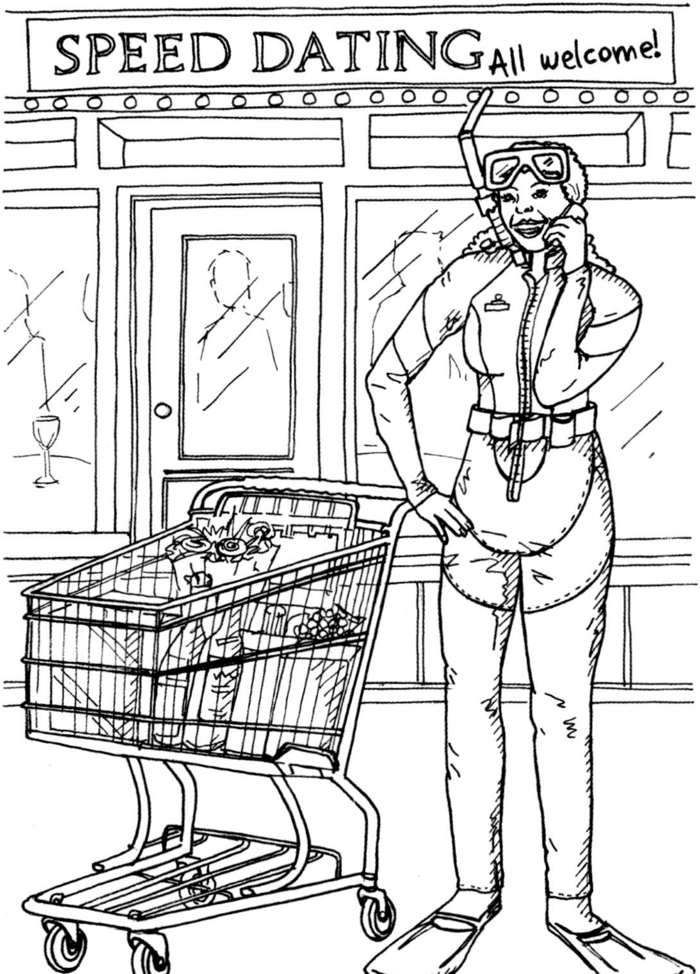
SPEED DATING
All welcome!

chapter 1
Finding love

Many of us spend most of our waking moments, consciously or not, looking for love. Often in the wrong places and usually with methods that are almost guaranteed to sabotage our efforts before we even begin.

Over the years as an agony aunt, counsellor, presenter of television relationship programmes—and of course someone who has herself danced the dance of love—I have picked up more than my fair share of tips on the How, Where, When and Why of meeting people. I have watched others and learned from their mistakes, and I have observed myself and learned from mine. I have read the great and the good and spoken with the wise and wonderful around the globe. What have I learned? Well you're about to find out...

How to meet new people

The easiest way is to open yourself up to the possibility. 'All the good ones are taken' or any of those phrases you'll hear around the makeup counter at the shopping centre guarantee failure. When I say to people 'You're a good one and you're not taken!' they usually mumble 'Well that's different'. Which I assume translates to 'Actually I'm not a good one but maybe I'll be able to fool someone into thinking I am'. You may not be perfect but that's OK because neither is anyone else. Somewhere out there is someone who has the same proportion of pluses and minuses as you and think how much fun you can have finding them!

Increasing your options

Keep yourself open to meeting all sorts of new people. The more people you meet the greater the chance you'll meet someone. One of the biggest mistakes that we make is to restrict ourselves to the types of new people we want to meet. We only want to meet men, or women, or people of this age or that religion or the other background. Not so. *Meet everyone!* Young, old, married, single, male, female. Just because the person standing in front of you isn't the type of person you currently envisage as your future partner doesn't mean that person isn't lurking around in their circle of friends and acquaintances. Be open, be friendly, and find out what is interesting about each person that you meet. Ask them about themselves, tell them about you and in no time you'll find that you're meeting new people and making new friends — that's when you'll meet that certain someone.

Where to meet new people

Where is the best place to meet people? On the bus, at a wedding, in the supermarket — I've known people to meet new partners at funerals. *Any time or place that has more than one person present is a possible opportunity to meet someone.* Longer working hours, busier lives, distance from our families and no longer living in prescribed communities, have contributed to some of the difficulties we now face regarding meeting new people. However some ingenious solutions have come into play and it has never been easier if you're willing to give it a go ...

Friends

Meeting people through friends has always been a good method. **PROS:** Chances are you will already have shared interests and values. Often you'll be able to observe each other from a distance before taking the step of spending time together away from the group. **CONS:** You have to be *really* careful with these types of relationships, if it goes wrong you may cause rifts within the group. Meeting through friends is brilliant when it works, but can be disastrous when it doesn't – so tread carefully.

Family

I once did a television series based on whether or not your friends and family could pick a better partner for you than you would pick yourself. Guess what? Often they can. Your family knows and loves you – warts and all – and they are more likely to be capable of knowing what you *need* rather than what you *want*. Though nothing is more excruciatingly embarrassing than when on your 30th birthday your mother (who is even more desperate than you at this point) drags someone home from the Tesco parking lot that she 'just knew you would love because he looks *just* like that nice boy from Boyzone...'

At work

When I first started working my grandmother gave me an invaluable bit of advice. 'Don't relieve yourself in the same location in which you eat' – which loosely translates to 'don't go out with people you work with'. I have lived in the UK for over 15 years and am *still* arguing this point with people. 'Where else am I to meet people?' Hopefully after reading this book you won't need to ask that question anymore. More than any other kind of relationship this is the one that cannot help but be fraught with peril. If it goes right you run the risk of losing the respect of your co-workers, damaging your chances for promotion (especially if you're female) and becoming the focus of everyone's water-cooler chats.

If the relationship ends—which often they do—then it can get singularly unpleasant. My mailbag is constantly filled with letters and emails along the lines of 'I was dating this guy in my office now we've split up and he's telling everyone my private business'. Usually someone who dates once in an office will make a habit of it. So when your dalliance ends chances are you're going to have to sit there and watch him sneaking off to the supply closet with someone else. Yes it is possible to meet the love of your life anywhere. But *please* try your best that it be anywhere other than work.

Internet

The past ten years has seen meeting on the Internet overtake just about any other form of hooking-up out there. Initially most people met through chat rooms (a virtual 'room' where people with a common interest chat in a group) — many still do. Then came dating sites, discussion forums, social networking sites and all are flourishing. I have attended weddings that sprang from meetings on the Internet and christenings of babies born from people who met on an Internet site and decided maybe touching each other might be more enjoyable than a keyboard.

Recently I went to lunch with a woman from the North of England who I had met on a discussion forum. She had come to London to have tea with the Queen; contrary to the-nerd-with-no-life image of netheads you really do meet all sorts. I have even engaged in a spot of internet romance myself. The inter-net works well for a culture where many of us are still slightly reserved. It gives you a chance to get to know people in a more gentle way than being flung into the deep end of your local pub on a Saturday night. It is a boon for those of us who live in areas that are relatively isolated and a Godsend for those of us who have issues around childcare. It brings you together with people who are like minded souls in a fairly effective way.

Type in 'fond of Hungarian goulash' and you will instantly access a couple thousand folks within shouting distance who feel the same way. If you're a bit on the shy side I advise going to sites that are about a shared interest rather than 'here's my picture do you like the look of me?' All the normal 'don't give out personal information, don't meet up with strangers in unsafe locations, be honest in your descriptions' guidelines do apply.

Personal ads

There is a marvellous book called *Round Heeled Woman* about a woman in her 60s who ran a personal ad and then spent the following year keeping company with the various gentlemen who responded. For the literary amongst us with a good turn of phrase, personal ads can be the way to go. However first you have to get past the vernacular: GSOH (Good Sense of Humour), DWK (Divorced With Kids), and FC (Follically Challenged – bald). Then you have to decide where to place the ad. Are you a Guardian reader, The Spectator, The Sun? – Whichever publication you read, chances are they have a personal ads section. You pay to place the ad; they give you a contact location (number, post box, or email address) through which the respondents contact you. You decide which responses are appealing and begin a corre-spondence. With the advent of the Internet, personal ads are not as popular as they used to be but for the faint hearted it is easier as the pace is slower.

Speed dating

Definitely for the brave! A group of people meet in a large room where there are individual tables with chairs on either side. A timer is set for, usually, 5 minutes and you have a chance to make whatever impression you can on the person on the other side of the table. The whistle blows and you move on to the next table. And so on and so on. At the end of the evening a moderator tallies the scores and you find out who would like to possibly get to know you better. Speed dating can be fun if you go in a group or if you don't take it too seriously. Go to a session where you will be with similar people to yourself. I once observed a session of young investment professionals and it was like sharks at a feeding frenzy. Speed dating originally came out of the Orthodox Jewish community as a way for young people to meet each other while staying with the bounds of propriety – it has certainly moved on a long way since then!

Social clubs

These can occur in a variety of guises. Everything from Young Farmers of Wales to Followers of Star Trek will have a club with meetings, activities, excursions and sometimes even grownup things like insurance policies. There are also social clubs as in louche, but delightful, membership clubs in most of the big cities. You pay a yearly membership fee, there is usually a regular location and for those who don't like pubs and wine bars it can be a very civilised place to relax and meet people. Social clubs tend to have a general theme, not always officially identified, which can be anything from people who work in the media to people who grow petunias. Check what sort of people you are going to be lounging around the fireplace with before you join.

> Confidence is
> the sexiest thing
> a woman can have.
> It's much sexier
> than any body part.

Aimee Mullins

Activities

For my money this might be the best way to meet people; possibly because it always worked for me.

Think of something you would like to learn, find a place that has a course in it, sign up for the course and you're away. The benefit of this method is that if you don't meet anyone you will still walk away with a magnificent piece of pottery or a horse's head that you sculpted yourself. Commonsense is appropriate here. If you are looking for a big hairy outdoorsy bloke then perhaps a lace-making course is not the way to go, nor is 'How to do acrylic nails at home'. If there isn't anything you want to learn then join a club that does something that you enjoy like rambling or bike riding. It is a lot less pressured when you do something with a group of people who share an interest – you're engaging in an activity you already like doing and if you meet someone, well, that's an added bonus!

Dating agencies

A comprehensive form profiling your personality and what you're looking for is filled out by you. A fee is exchanged – which can be anything from £50 to £10,000 (and don't assume the higher the fee the better the service). Then the nice people who work at the dating agency will look though their client list and see who they have on their register who most matches up with your data and what you are looking for. They will choose a small selection, usually about three or four, they will then send you mini-dossiers on the people and you can choose whether or not. It makes total sense, and it does work for many, however there are three things you need to watch out for.

The first is that you need to be totally honest when filing

out your application and so do they. Descriptive phrases are sometimes used with reckless abandon by the ladies so watch out for words like 'slim', 'young', 'blonde'. While the gentlemen sometimes get a bit carried away with phrases referring to their finances so 'almost millionaire' (yes I have seen that) and 'financially solvent' can often mean just the opposite. Also be aware that often if someone is stumping up a lot of money for such a service it might mean they are overly zealous in their search – if that doesn't pose a problem for you then this method might work for you.

Last, but probably most important, is the ability of the people running the dating service to appreciate you as an individual and not just match you up with another set of comparable ticked boxes. I have seen some spectacular successes from dating agencies so if you're really serious then give it a try but remember to interview the agency thoroughly before plunking down your hard-earned cash.

When to meet new people

Anytime can be the right time to meet people. For some reason there seems to be an idea that Meeting People is a specific activity. We are going out to 'meet people' is the cry heard as the weekend rolls around. You can meet people *anytime*. However this conversation is probably more about when **not** to meet people. Many of us look at love as the cure-all for any of life's ills so at the first sign of trouble on the horizon we fling ourselves into finding love. We're bored – it's time to meet someone. We have a real issue that needs dealing with and meeting someone becomes a diversion to keep you away from the real task at hand. Then there are the folk who immediately upon the ending of a relationship decide 'Yes, right — let's rush right out and find a replacement'. For the record that is the absolute *worst* time to go looking for love.

Almost anytime can be a good time to meet people; just do a quick MOT on yourself. Check that you really are in the right frame of mind for something that while enjoyable and rewarding can also be taxing. In other words — don't put on the uniform if you don't really have the energy for the game.

What to keep in mind

Many of us launch ourselves into the dating world with the purposefulness of Napoleon planning a military campaign. There is an air of grim determination that I have seen on the faces of people accompanied by the dreaded phrase 'I just **have** to meet someone'. The look in their eyes would be guaranteed to scare the life out of anyone who may accidentally come across their path; and the phrase 'deer in headlights' certainly springs to mind. Nothing scares people away more than feeling that they are a trophy to be acquired. People want to come towards you naturally not be dragged by force. Keep in mind that the law of nature is such that what you search for most diligently is often the most difficult to find. Think of it as looking for fun. Start out with the concept that you are hoping to meet someone with similar interests and outlook as yourself. Then add on 'someone I am attracted to who is attracted to me', 'someone I want to get to know better'. If there is really something there it will grow naturally. There is nothing that will throw a spanner in the works faster than two people meeting each other, there is a small attraction and one launches into a mission to ensnare the other at all costs. If it's real, it will happen.

Asking someone out

In my experience I have never heard of anything particularly disastrous happening to someone who asked a person out on a date. There are basically two things that can happen: **1)** They say 'yes'... or 2) They say 'no'. Most of us tend to totally ignore the possibility of it being a 'yes' and focus totally on *it-will-be-no-and-lightning-will-strike-me-down-and-I-shall-be-humiliated-for-the-rest-of-my-life*. First let's not forget that you often get what you focus on. Approaching the situation with the hope of a positive outcome is more likely to gain you a positive outcome.

Next let's keep in mind that the world will not end if the person says no. It does not mean you are a bad person, an unattractive person, a dislikeable person. Neither does it mean that no one will ever like you and you are destined to spend your life on the scrapheap of life. It just means that at this particular time this particular person is not inclined. Here are a few pointers to ease the process of asking someone out:

1 Don't think about it for 6 months while you try to get up the courage. *Just do it!*

2 Don't discuss it with all your family, friends, and the postman. *Just do it!*

3 Don't do it in front of other people or in a public place with all your friends and their friends standing around watching.

4 If possible, maybe you're shy, there is nothing wrong with asking by email or text. By the way while it is acceptable to ask by these methods it is never acceptable to cancel by these methods.

5 Keep it simple and to the point 'I was wondering if you would be interested in going for a cup of coffee some time?'.

Before the date

Keep in mind that this is just a date, nothing more – nothing less. For a brief period of time two people are going to engage in activities which they both enjoy. You will attempt to get to know more about each other. This is NOT a-job-interview-to-determine-the-outcome-of-the-rest-of-your-life; so chill out. Don't overthink the date. I am constantly hearing from people 'I met him/her, I thought we would get along and we went on a date and she was a totally different person. What a nut-job!'.

It's difficult but try not to discuss your upcoming date with the entire world. You may be proud, excited, nervous – but the more people you discuss it with before is the more people you'll have to discuss it with after. Wait until you know if there is anything to talk about before blabbing to all and sundry.

Wear comfortable clothing. Ladies try on your outfits before you go. Walk around the house for half an hour. If you have to hold in your stomach, tug it up, tug it down, can't breathe in it then for heaven's sake don't wear it. 'She spent the whole night tugging her skirt down, what was that all about?' Comfortable shoes are also a good idea. It might sound to you that I am saying go in your jimjams and slippers – I am not. However, unless you are going on a job interview as a lap dancer, there is no need to present yourself as one. Especially on first dates when you're not yet certain of what sort of relationship you want to have. Don't advertise something that might not be on offer.

During the date (yes)

One of the secrets to having people like you in any situation is for you to make them feel better about themselves for having spent time with you. How does one do that? By paying attention to them. Asking questions and listening to their answers. Asking more questions based on what they've said (which makes them realise that you've been listening). Find out what they're interested in. What music they like. How they spend their spare time. Where they like to go on holiday.

However be careful how you do this. Don't make it seem like you're going down a checklist. Avoid questions like 'What sort of car do you drive?' and 'Do you have a pension fund?' Stay positive – I know that is difficult for some of us but give it a whirl. No one likes a whinger but yet we're all willing to be one. Save that for when you've already endeared yourself to them! I know people who have spent their entire first date discussing the merits of Snow Patrol over Coldplay or Tom Jones over Tony Bennett. Most importantly – be yourself.

During the date (no)

Don't rabbit on endlessly about yourself. Don't ask questions that sound as if you're a bank officer and they are applying for a mortgage. Do NOT ask questions about their past relationships – there will be time enough for that later. Do NOT volunteer information about your past relationships. Why so many people feel the need to do this I will never understand. Trust me, no good ever comes of it. It creates the impression that you are either bitter or bringing unnecessary baggage to the table.

I suspect that very few of you will listen to me but I'm going to say it anyway – limit your alcohol consumption. If you feel that you can easily handle six glasses of wine – then keep it to three. If three is your number then stick to one. I have yet to meet anyone who is more interesting when under-the-influence. You may think you are but trust me you probably aren't. Do you ever wonder why so many relationships fall down at the three month mark? Often that is around the first time that the parties involved spend time together without alcohol being involved. In the cold light of day they realise they're actually not really that interested. Unless you've got three months to waste try not to be off your trolley for your first couple of dates.

After the date (yes)

You've had a good time. You think the other person has had a good time. What happens next? First of all at the end of the date be sure to say thank you (even if you've had an awful time – it's only polite). I know it sounds like an accepted fact but you wouldn't believe how many people don't do it, so don't forget to say 'Thank you'.

If you really like the person and would like to see them again it is completely acceptable to say so. 'Thank you, I really enjoyed myself maybe we can do it again sometime'. Make sure to say it like a casual statement rather than 'ask me on another date right now why don't you?' That could make the other person uncomfortable and feel as if they're being put on the spot. If you are too shy to say it then feel comfortable to email or text. However you do it, carrier pigeon or skywriting – be sure to let them know you've enjoyed yourself and would not be averse to repeating the experience.

After the date (no)

First check the entry directly above. As mentioned it is a big no-no not to give an indication as to whether or not the date was a success from your point of view. But the biggest no-no of all is saying you'll call if you have no intention in the world of doing so. That is really unkind and leaves the person on tenterhooks waiting for something that isn't going to happen. Be honest, which does NOT mean 'This was the worst night of my life and I wouldn't go out with you again if you were the last person on earth'. A simple 'Thank you for tonight and good luck with your job interview' is polite but carries no promise of further contact that you do not intend to carry through.

Another no-no is discussing your thoughts with anyone who may know the person. Comments like 'watching paint dry', or 'what a loser!' have a way of getting back to the person some-how. It might be true, but you wouldn't like it done unto to you so don't do it unto them.

Falling in love with friends

One of the most common phenomena these days is people falling in love with close friends. It could be someone you went to university with, a flatmate, a best friend's brother – you've been going on holiday together, hanging out together and all of a sudden one day you look up and decide 'uh-oh....I think I like him in That Way!' One of the reasons this happens frequently nowa-days is that many of us build walls around ourselves to protect against the people we feel we could possibly have a relationship with. We have our defence systems in place against people we don't want to hurt us (potential partners), but are completely open to people we feel safe with (our friends). As this person gets

"I've been on so
many blind dates,
I should get
a free dog.

Wendy Leibman

to see the natural-100% you it is possible to know each other and develop a walls-down-closeness that might feel like something slightly more than 'just friends'.

Think *very carefully* before you make such a move and move very slowly. Allow yourself the room to step back if needs be without having made a total mess of the friendship. Try to keep bedroom antics out of the equation (at least until you are absolutely sure) – that's the step that is most difficult to retreat from with a shred of dignity if it doesn't work out. Difficult but not impossible, I've seen friends cross the line then cross back safely. I've also seen people who were friends for years finally realise that the very thing they had been searching the world for was right under their noses all along.

'Wrong' relationships

We've all had at least one inappropriate relationship – some more 'wrong' than others. The 17-year-old boy at the local green-grocers, your ex's sister, your boss – the new vicar. My advice, from my advanced years, is to resist the temptation and don't do it. But if you're young and invincible you're not going to want to listen; and if you're not so young and have made a lifetime habit of this then you're not going to want to listen either. So if you have convinced yourself that despite obvious indications to the contrary this person is The One just do us both a small favour and ask yourself these five questions first:

1   Why is this an inappropriate relationship? Who would categorise it in that way?

2   Who would be hurt if I go ahead with it?

3 What are the moral/legal/social implications of going ahead with it?

4 What changes will it make to my life if I follow my heart (or whichever body part is leading you)?

5 Is it really worth it?

Odds are that when you've asked yourself these questions you will decide that maybe it isn't such a great idea after all. However if after seriously thinking about it you decide that it is the right thing to do then I wish you luck. Some wonderful lifetimes have grown from 'He's too old for her', 'She's from the wrong kind of family', 'They'll never last'. But **be careful...**

Chapter summary:

Pocket Primer – Meeting People

1. The more pressure you put on yourself, the more difficult the process will be.

2. Stay positive – you will attract what you believe is out there.

3. Stay open to all possibilities.

4. Believe in what you have to offer.

5. Be yourself – be honest and stay natural.

The biggest problem most of us have in regards to meeting new people and starting relationships is that we go into it with a long list of who it should be, when it should be, where it should be, and exactly how it should happen. The best thing you can do for yourself is lose those thoughts. Love is a force like no other with its own ideas as to when it will show up, where it will show up, and in what guise it will present itself. Leave yourself free to be surprised and I guarantee you will be.

Lots of people want to ride with you in the limo, but what you want is someone who will take the bus with you when the limo breaks down.

Oprah Winfrey

Helping
love grow

chapter 2
Helping love grow

Before we start we tend to believe that the difficult bit is 'getting a partner'. That we'll 'catch' someone and the difficult bit is over. Tee-hee! It's just the beginning. A relationship is an ongoing process. We think the whole process of finding someone is a big complicated activity and after you've caught them well if it's a good relationship it will just work out all by itself. Guess what, it just isn't so. Now is when the hard work really begins. Putting on a bit of lip-gloss or delivering a snappy chat-up line is easy; it's building on all this that is the challenge.

One of the tricks to a good relationship is finding two people whose wants and needs are fairly similar and who are both willing to put in the necessary work to turn the situation from 'just dating' to a proper relationship. Keep in mind that Rome was not built in a day so don't expect the perfect relationship overnight. It might be a bit bumpy in the beginning but the work must be done and fingers crossed it will be worth it.

Moving the relationship on

There comes a moment when you realise that maybe this is something more than a casual friendship. Something alters your routine and you don't see each other as often as you usually do and you miss her like crazy. Or he mentions a new girl working in his office and you feel a stab of jealousy. Whatever the signals you realise that you might want more from this person than you currently have. You want to take the relationship to another level.

Firstly sit down and think this through. What kind of relationship are you looking for? Where do you want to end up? Have you gotten any signals from the other person indicating they might feel the same?

Initiate this progression by planning an activity you've not indulged in before. Going away for a weekend, meeting your close friends, are just the kind of thing that indicate a relationship is moving into new territory. Suggest doing something at a point a couple of months away—booking tickets for an exhibition or concert—see how the suggestion is received. If there is an uncomfortable silence and flimsy excuses then back down for the time being. If the suggestion is greeted positively then you're on the right track.

Consider carefully

Decide if you truly believe the relationship has legs. Do you want to move the relationship along because your 38th birthday is rapidly approaching, it's the best sex you've ever had, it's easier than looking for someone else OR do you want to move the relationship along because you have very special feelings for this particular person.

Ask yourself this

Here are a few questions to ask yourself before you make the final decision.

1 Would you say your attraction to this person is more physical than mental?

2 Is there anyone else in the world you would rather be with?

3 Do you trust this person?

4 Are you comfortable in this person's company?

5 If you close your eyes and try to imagine the rest of your life without this person, how do you feel?

Answer these questions carefully and you should end up with a very accurate portrayal of the situation.

Making your feelings known

This is the tricky bit and what we are most afraid of but *it has to be done*. Some people, like me, can be read like a book. If I like someone they will know because it is written all over my face – couldn't hide it if I wanted to, believe me there have been times when I have tried. But not everyone is an open book so you cannot sit there quietly assuming that the other person knows how deep your true feelings are. I know this is difficult. You are putting yourself on the line, opening yourself up to possible hurt, and putting yourself in the most vulnerable position possible.

It is important that you move forward at a rate with which you are comfortable. Sometimes a look is worth a thousand words. Take the person's hand, look into their eyes and say '*You know I really like you*' and smile. Might sound odd but it works. You want to open the door to a conversation, not necessarily make a grand declaration; there will be time enough for that later.

Ask him/her

This is a step for the brave, but if you can it could save you a lot of heartache down the road. It's really important that both parties are singing from the same hymn sheet. It is crucial that one of you isn't thinking that moving the relationship on means spending a bit more time together – while the other feels that you've stepped on the movable sidewalk which will deposit you both at the altar. You must decide what this change in circumstance means to you and the other person; for example will you continue to see other people?

Check your direction

It isn't about making demands or issuing ultimatums but it is about making sure you're both heading in the same direction. In any decent relationship there will be plateaus and rites of passage. The first time you meet a family member, the first time you go on holiday. If there are children from a previous relationship then there's the first time you're introduced to them. It isn't necessary or possible to establish right at the beginning what the route is going to be that the two of you will take. But it is important that you have a strong sense that you are both interested in going in the same direction.

When parties have different views

When someone says 'He'll come around I'm sure of it', my heart falls to the floor. Millions of relationships from the beginning of time have been based on this concept. One person states what they are expecting to do or be a part of. The other is diametrically opposed but has complete faith that it will only take time and the other party will come to their senses. Yes, people do some-

I love being married. It's so great to find that one special person you want to annoy for the rest of your life.

Rita Rudner

times change their mind, but usually they don't. Sometimes the person who said they really didn't ever plan on getting married really meant it. The person who said no to children might really mean it. You are setting yourself up for an almighty crash if you go into a relationship with the idea that you are going to change the other person and ignore their beliefs. Take people as you find them, if they change then you're lucky but don't count on it. If them staying the way they are or holding on to the beliefs that they currently have will cause untold difficulties then walk away now.

Taking the next step

If you are just going to spend more time together then there isn't really anything to be done. You might want to decide between you if you need to make a semi-official announcement to your friends. Terrible rows have come out of one person telling the world and the other one wanting it to be a secret. If you are doing something as monumental as moving in together then it is crucial that you both communicate clearly what your expectations are. Several big conversations need to be had and guidelines put in place and agreed to. This is especially important if you will be taking actions that will involve finances, but more on that in the section on money. Don't be put off though as this is one of the loveliest times in a new relationship. The slate is clean, everything is sparkling and shiny and the world is your oyster.

The role of communication

If I had to choose one element that can make or break a relationship it would be communication. The business of how we go about making our thoughts, feelings, likes, dislikes, troubles, joys and any other emotion you can think of, known to others. How we put forth these things and how we receive them from other folk is possibly the biggest determination as to the quality of life you enjoy in any arena but in this more than any other.

First let's define communication. If I were to ask you what that means many of you would say 'telling folk what I think'. That is only a small part of communication. It is crucial when beginning a relationship that you discuss your methods of communicating. If you are a shouter then you must say *'Listen sometimes I get a bit loud but I really don't mean it. If it bothers you then let me know'*. If you're someone who holds it in *'Listen sometimes it takes me awhile to let it out but be patient I'll get there eventually'*. I cannot underscore enough how important it is to get this right. Many a good relationship has fallen by the wayside due to poor communication; don't let yours be one of them.

The role of trust

One of the most important building blocks of any relationship is trust. It is trust in this other person that provides you with the feeling of security that most of us are looking for in a relationship. And without it there will be that constant feeling of dis-ease. When I ask people 'Do you trust him?' you would be surprised how many people cheerfully say 'Not on your Nelly!' This isn't good and it isn't healthy.

Ask yourself this – what is it that you don't trust the person about? Do you not trust them to be faithful? Do you not trust them to be truthful? Is it money that you don't trust them about? Do you not trust them to stay with you? Is it all of the above or do you just feel that it is inevitable that they will at some point hurt you badly so you'll just sit patiently waiting for it to happen.

Watch your focus

I am now going to say something that might upset some of you – and I will repeat it throughout this book. In my experiences, both personal and professional, *you tend to get what you focus on*. If you go around expecting the worst, chances are the worst will happen. Yes, you usually cannot prove that it may not have happened if you hadn't focussed on it; but do us all a favour and focus on your relationship working and working brilliantly and then go for it. (*See Forgive and forget.)

Choosing your battles

When most of our mothers were young the rule of thumb was that a good wife is obedient. She listens to the head of the household (the man), she doesn't cause trouble. Things have changed and the past couple of decades have taught us that swallowing your anger is extremely unhealthy – both for your body and your mind. However constantly ranting and raving is also no good for anyone. It weakens your relationship and is very distressing for your children. I am constantly coming across children whose main wish is for their parents to **just stop** arguing. It makes them feel unsettled and insecure.

To argue or not to argue?

What do you do when you are bothered? Where is the line between expressing your negative feelings in a constructive fashion and burying them? First of all learn how to choose your battles. Everything doesn't need to be a cause for a row. When you see something that bothers you ask yourself 'How serious is this? Is it really worth making a fuss about?' 'Can I change my attitude about it so that it doesn't really bother me?' If you can't, then mention it but in a non-confrontational way, and don't wait until you are about to explode.

How to argue effectively

'All married couples should learn the art of battle as they should learn the art of making love. Good battle is objective and honest, never vicious or cruel. Good battle is healthy and constructive and brings to a marriage the principle of equal partnership.' Ann Landers

The make-or-break factor

How disagreements are handled within a relationship can be one of the strongest determining factors as to whether or not the relationship works in the long term. In the main the more displaced or emotionally distant a topic, the more a man is willing to argue it. He will argue himself into a blue fit over who is the better goalie. But try to have a heated discussion about how hurt your feelings were when he forgot your birthday and many a man will be as quiet as a church mouse. Of course it is no surprise that we women also have our issues. We often tend to turn things better ignored into a matter of life-or-death-of-the-relationship.

What outcome are you looking for?

It helps if you know from the beginning what you want the outcome to be. Do you want to solve the problem or are you just interested in having a row? If you're letting off steam then have your rant and say 'Right, well I just felt I needed to say that'. However I would advise against employing this tactic with any frequency because after awhile it could permanently damage your relationship.

But what if you're trying to resolve a specific issue and can see that this particular exchange is not getting anywhere or you just don't feel like talking anymore? Then *'It seems as if we aren't making any progress on this right now, how do you feel about ending this particular conversation about it and we can pick it up again when we're both up for it?'* You have very clearly expressed your feelings that this isn't going anywhere but that the matter has not yet been resolved and will need to be discussed further at another time.

Controlling your mood

A couple of points to keep in mind. If you really want a resolve then don't shout. Nothing inflames a situation like raised voices. Be forceful if necessary but remain measured and calm. Don't say you're sorry if you don't mean it. That just makes you angry inside which will eventually then cause yet another argument. Too much arguing is no good but no arguing at all can be even worse. So you must do it, but please do it well.

How to make up

Don't go to sleep not speaking. If you can't resolve the issue then after acknowledging that you're not going to take it any further at this particular point in time say *'Present circumstances aside, I do love you'*. Or something simpler like *'Have a good night'*. There are some people who feel that the best way to make up from an argument is something material like flowers or chocolates or extra sex. ☻ For some this might work (especially the latter) but what most people, especially women, are really looking for is an indication that you genuinely regret whatever has happened.

Ways to apologise

The other party will also want an indication when you apologise, and you should, that you intend making a staunch effort that it will not happen again. If talking about emotional stuff isn't easy for you then the shops are full to overflowing with 'Roses are red violets are blue I sure am sorry I acted like poo-poo' cards. Buy one. Believe it or not that will often work better than a very impersonal gift.

If you've really pulled a big one then plan an activity that you know will mean something to other person. It could be something big but you'll find that cooking his favourite dinner or running her a candlelit bath can reinforce the fact that you are sorry. Simple phrases like 'I really do appreciate you' and 'I really am sorry' then move on and get back on track with the relationship.

Talking about money

A few years ago some research came out that said that the biggest reason couples were splitting up wasn't infidelity but finances. Granted the research might have been commissioned by a bank but the fact is that for a lot of the couples who come through my doors, finances, and how they are handled or mis-handled, is at the centre of their difficulties. It is very important that in a relationship no one feels like they're being treated like a child especially in relationship to finances. It is also important that no one feels as if they're being taken advantage of.

The tone of finances in a relationship is usually set in the very beginning. So as embarrassing or difficult as it might be for some of us to discuss it, we must. In our culture we would prefer to talk about anything other than money so we tend to either not bring it up, or say yes to whatever is mooted whether or not we really

"A good marriage is one which allows for change and growth in the individuals and in the way they express their love."

Pearl Buck

agree. Don't do this. You must state clearly from the beginning what you really feel as it will cause nothing but grief down the road if you don't. Saying 'Well actually I wasn't comfortable with that but didn't want to say' after the fact is definitely going to exacerbate the problem.

Getting outside help

Sometimes it helps to bring a third party into the conversation. In every library, bookshop, and on Amazon you can now find workbooks on finances. Get one. Sit down with a bottle of wine and a couple of pencils and make up a plan to order your finances. As time goes by and your relationship grows there will be more and more expenses and serious financial stuff to deal with. It is very important that you get into the habit of talking about it in an open fashion from the beginning. It is much better to build a solid foundation in the beginning than to later spend money on repairs.

The role of exes

How easy life would be if we didn't have exes but the fact is that we all will have a couple of them buried somewhere in the shed. I believe the less said about one's exes the better. No good ever comes of it but I know as well as I am sitting here that you're not going to listen to me. I shall say 'Talk at your own peril'. It will be a rare man or woman who can overcome the urge in the middle of an argument to say 'No wonder he left you' or 'That woman you've been calling crazy wasn't crazy at all, you really are a co-dependent mama's boy'.

Discussing your past relationships

While I strongly believe that you shouldn't volunteer information on your past relationships, I also believe that you shouldn't lie. 'So what did your last relationship die of?' – *Really* **Bad** Answer: *'He cheated on me with my best mate. I always used to tell him that I thought he would cheat on me and he did. I was glad to see the back of him because he was rubbish in bed and anyway he didn't want to get married or have children so what use was he?'* Really **Good** Answer: *'We just had different paths in mind and thought it better that we go our separate ways. Anyway this merlot really is tasty where did you buy it?'* I suspect there's not a snowball in hell's chance that you're going to do the latter but for my sake can we aim for somewhere in between the two?

Dealing with jealousy

Other issues of exes can be things like your new partner being jealous of the past relationship, the amount of time you still spend with the ex, or if they have the feeling that you're still not completely clear of the relationship and there is a chance you will go back to the person.

Hand on heart is there cause for worry? If not then here are a couple of things you can do.

1   Ask your new partner what it is they are afraid of? *'That isn't going to happen because I am with you now. Don't forget that I broke up with them before I met you and already knew beyond a shadow of doubt that the relationship was over.'*

2   Make a list of the things you prefer about your new love and tell them what they are *'Sam was OK, but you're fabulous because a-b-c...... I am so happy to be with you because I've*

always wanted to be with someone who could build a fire by rubbing two sticks together.'

Topics to avoid

I happen to believe that a *tiny* bit of jealousy can be healthy. But if this person starts trying to control your behaviour then watch out; this inclination to control you might rear its ugly head in other areas as well. Men – here's a tip: *never* EVER answer questions about an ex's appearance and if possible I would also avoid showing photographs. There is nothing more competitive than a woman.

Many a tear has been shed 'She's way more beautiful than me, he'll never stay with me after being with someone who looks like her etc.etc.etc.' And boys don't be fooled! Any question, however innocent, really translates to 'Was she prettier, sexier, had a bigger bust/smaller bum than me?' Don't fall for it! Ladies – under **no** circumstance answer any sex questions about your previous relationships. 'It was ok/alright' is the only appropriate answer.

The role of children and their parents

It isn't easy to find someone these days without a child; especially men over the age of about 34. If you do then consider yourself lucky. It is a sad indication of many aspects of our society that there are so many splintered families; but it is a reality and one just has to deal with it. It is a generalisation but usually when a man hooks up with a woman the obstacle he perceives as needing to get over are the children. When a woman hooks up with a man with a past it's the ex-wife that is more likely to cause her sleepless nights.

The distinction between ex-partner and mother/father-of-my-child

There is usually a marked difference in how one reacts if you yourself have been married before. You will tend to be more reasonable about the expectations of your new partner's former partner. You know that no matter what the current circumstance they will always be tied together as parents of their children. Sometimes it is very difficult for single people to understand this so if you're a parent and your new partner has never been one then it is important that you have a conversation about your role as a parent. Often people get confused and think that the constant visits to the house where your children reside means that you still are deeply in love with their mother.

Clarifying your role as a parent

You must lay your cards on the table with your new partner; *'Emily and I aren't together anymore because we were just not right for each other BUT I am still a hands-on father to Bobby and Susannah. I see them every Sunday afternoon and on holidays. I will try my best not to let it impinge on our relationship but they are my kids and I am very committed to them.'* You've laid your cards on the table and chances are you will have made a good impression with your new girl. If however she doesn't understand or kicks up a fuss, well it's for you to decide, but I would find such an attitude worrisome.

When you're a mother

If you're a mother and in a new relationship then your issues are twofold. There is the 'When do I introduce him to the idea of the children?' 'When do I introduce the children to the idea of him?'

I'm sure I don't need to tell you not to hide the fact that you have children. If you were the sort of person who would do that then you probably wouldn't be reading this book. But just in case – do NOT under any circumstance do that. Many a man has gotten up from the table and walked away not because a woman has children (as she will tell all her friends) but more likely because she lied about it. Mention quite quickly that you have two children; but don't talk about them constantly; there'll be time enough for that later. Give the relationship a chance to grow first.

Dealing with a difficult ex

If either of you gets stuck with a difficult ex then you do have my sympathies. What you do about it depends on how you see the future of your current relationship. I have known of women who have taken difficult exes out for coffee and given the '*Your children are really wonderful, you are so lucky to have them; anything I can do to help make your job easier please let me know/they will always only have one mother and I respect that*' speech. I've yet to hear an instance when it didn't have the desired effect.

Communication – your new partner and their children

You should never restrict the communication between a parent and their children. But if you have the sense that the parent/ex is just trying to cause disruption then it is completely within your right to say so. If you find that the parent is calling three or four times a night and demanding your current partner then it might be necessary to have the '*Do you mind asking her whenever possible to call during the day or between 7 and 7.30 or 10 and 10.30*' conversation.'

As this type of extended-family relationship becomes more common we seem to be coming up with more effective was of handling it. I am constantly meeting families where you can't figure out where the 'old' children end and the 'new' begin. And have been to several dinners where 'Oh and this is the mother of Ella and Samuel...' and no one bats an eyelash. It can be done and is best for all.

The role of families

This can depend on how old you are, your background or your relationship with your family. It can also depend on the nature of your relationship and where you see it heading.

The role of your new partner's family

When I was young, free, and single I had no thoughts one way or another as to what someone's family was like. When I got a bit older and started thinking of building a proper relationship with someone then their family became a very important part of the equation. What sort of relationship did they have with their family? How much input did their family have in their day to day lives? Were there things about the other person's family that might impact on our relationship such as religious differences etc.? To some people these things don't matter at all. I have to say that to me they did. I wasn't willing to marry into a family where the difference in our backgrounds could possibly cause a problem for our children. Times have moved on since then and those kinds of issues are usually less of a worry than they were; unless you come from a family that strictly observes certain religious guidelines.

Parents who think their offspring are still children

Nowadays you're more likely to have problems with an overprotective father who thinks no one is good enough for his little princess – even if said princess is 38. And of course the mother who feels that no Mazda-driving smart-aleck career woman (who has probably slept with half the Home Counties) is going to iron her son's socks with the same attention to detail that she has for the past 40 years, never mind raise her precious grandchildren in accordance with her rules. How you respond to all this will often depend on what kind of family you come from.

Mothers-in-law, handle with care

One of my closest friends is now dealing with mother-in-law from hell and I swear I don't know how she hasn't throttled the woman. On the other hand I have to say that my ex-mother-in-law is an angel from heaven and we remain firm friends, so don't always expect a mother-in-law to be the enemy.

Dealing with siblings

As far as siblings go try not to get involved in historical scraps – remain neutral, it's safest. Try not to drag someone away from their family but if there are aspects of the situation that you are uncomfortable with then feel free to say so. You are all adults and entitled to start your own life. I always suggest staying quietly on the outskirts of a new family in the early days and step in slowly and carefully – that's the safest way.

Marriage/Commitment

*For the sake of ease I am going to refer to everything in this section as 'marriage'. If commitment or civil partnership or whatever is more relevant for you then feel free to substitute.

The difference between a marriage and a wedding

If we're going to talk about marriage then let us first be clear that getting married is one thing – having a wedding is another. If having a wedding is the reason you're even thinking of this then for the love of Pete drop the idea *immediately*! A wedding is a party which lasts for only a few hours and the fun is over once you take the frock off. 'A husband is for life not just for Christmas' so act accordingly.

The legal benefits of getting hitched

Folk who are against marriage will often say 'It's only a bit of paper' or 'We don't like society telling us what to do'. Yet these are often the same people who complain that they don't have the same rights as married folk. I once had to do some research into the history of marriage and discovered to my surprise that marriage was not introduced because people were falling in love, or the church said you had to – that all came later.

The original purpose of marriage was to have a framework by which to disentangle unions if they went awry. That is why it used to only be rich folk who got married; and you didn't want some errant son-in-law keeping the half of Leicestershire that you had given him as a wedding present. So 'that bit of paper' is invaluable if you sadly come to disentangle your union as many a cohabiting couple has now found out. Never mind unmarried fathers who sadly have few or no legal rights at all.

Shed the fear and take the chance

But let's not dwell on the negative. 'What if it doesn't work out?' Where would we be as a civilisation if we never tried anything because we were afraid it might fail? However don't get married if you feel it guarantees you exemption from loneliness, money worries, or a childless future — it doesn't. Get married because you're not afraid of commitment and even more importantly if you're not afraid of failure.

Chapter summary:

Pocket Primer – Communication

1. **Get in the habit of saying positive things**. Some of us only open our mouths when we have something negative to say.

2. **Do not discuss your issues with all and sundry** before discussing them with the person in question. And if for some reason you decide to ignore this advice then please, please do not say 'Well I was talking to my mother about it and she thinks...' That is almost guaranteed to turn it from communication to argument.

3. **Don't be impatient**. Who knows how long it has taken the person initiating the conversation to begin. You care about this person and whatever they are about to say is probably, in their mind, for the good of the relationship.

4. If you don't understand what is being said to you or what the issue is then **ask for clarification**.

5. **Choose your times carefully**. Ladies, this does not mean right when he's about to fall asleep. Gentlemen, this does not mean while she is changing a nappy, looking for her briefcase, curling her eyelashes AND feeding the dog.

6. If you are the person initiating the conversation then be sure to **let the other person have their say as well**.

7. **Listen carefully to their response**. You might find it changes your perception of the issue.

8. Women tend to respond more intensely to tone and volume so **men please watch both**. On the other hand men tend to process information in short groups of words so **ladies don't waffle on**. Ten words and get to the point. Stop, let them absorb then deliver another ten words.

9. **Acknowledge the effort** the person has made to start this conversation. 'I know it must have been difficult for you to say this and I appreciate it.' And if you also feel 'I'm not sure if I agree but I'll take on board what you've said' then feel free to say so.

   If you're the person who started the conversation then 'Thank you for listening so patiently, I really needed to get this off my chest'.

10. **Speak regularly and often**. You would be surprised how little many couples talk these days. There is always one survey or another saying that it is six minutes a day or some other horrifying figure. Lack of communicating is one of the saddest things you often hear as a reason for couples drifting apart.

    Make a point each day of having even a short chat about something you want rather than have to talk about. Sounds simplistic but in the long run it's the little things that count.

Communication (cont)

Marriage isn't about trying to find the person you fancy the most then closing your eyes and hoping the feeling lasts for the rest of your life. That is a ridiculous and impractical expectation. Love grows and changes and that subtle difference you feel when you get married is due to its ebb and flow; the growth of an ever-strengthening bond. Like the tide there are times when you will think love has drained away then it will come flowing back and is all the sweeter for its return.

One day hopefully you will find the person who, when you close your eyes and try to imagine the rest of your life without them – you just can't. That is the feeling you're looking for. Then and only then is it the right time to say 'I do' and know you'll really mean it. There are no foolproof choices you can make in this life but if you truly believe then go for it.

"Don't smother each other. No one can grow in the shade.

Leo Buscaglia

Love is not enough.
It must be the
foundation, the
cornerstone – but not
the complete structure.
It is much too pliable,
too yielding.

Bette Davis

Keeping love alive

chapter 3
Keeping love alive

Yyou've made the commitment. You've walked down the aisle, gotten the mortgage, bought a dog, signed up for a family membership at the gym – or done whatever counts for a solid commitment in your world. You've cast your lot in with this person and most likely the plan is this is it – you'll be two old folks sitting on the bench in the park holding hands sharing a bag of chips.

How do you get from here to there? Are there steps you can take to guarantee that you'll end up with matching bus pass holders? I wish there was but sadly there are no guaranteed Ten Steps To Forever Together and it takes more than just wanting it to reach the finish line. Whenever I talk to couples who have been together forever the one thing they will always say 'It takes work but it's worth it'. In other words you do have to make an effort; but if you do the work there is a good chance you'll reap the rewards.

Conversely if you don't do the work, if you just sit there and think it will 'just happen' then don't be surprised at the results. That would be like planting a seedling, never watering it – then complaining when it doesn't grow into a tree.

Building on your dreams

1 Dedicate yourself to the relationship.

2 Don't willingly do things that you know will harm the relationship. It takes work, effort, maintenance.

3 Know each other's likes and dislikes.

4 Know what makes each other happy or sad.

5 Be loyal to each other.

6 Give each other the freedom and the time in which to maintain your individuality. Two wholes make a better unit.

7 Make sure the balance of power within the relationship regularly flows back and forth.

8 Do not treat each other with disrespect.

9 Take the extra time and make the extra effort to understand each other.

10 Take a minute each and every day to look each other in the eyes and say 'I love you'.

Keeping the relationship fresh

Did you know that being in love is actually an altered chemical state? Well it is. Many of us will experience clammy hands, racing pulse, butterflies in our tummies, and all sorts. Dopamine, Norepinephrine and Serotonin are the culprits that can have you obsessing over the object of your affection, planning to give up your job and move you both to a desert island, all and every form of insanity. You may also find yourself feeling disconnected when not in sight of your one true love. The good news is that this state of madness usually lasts for about 6-9 months. The bad news is that a lot of us expect it to last forever and when it ends we think the relationship is over.

Moving from lust to love

The truth of it is that in many ways this is when the relationship really begins. This is when we go from attraction to attachment, and it is attachment that will keep your relationship together. The chemicals your brain releases at this stage are oxytocin and vasopressin. Sadly they're not to be found in aisle 7 at the local chemist so it's not going to be possible to sprinkle a few vials over your partner's cornflakes and sit back. If you pay close attention to the pointers listed above you will be well ahead of the game but I want you to be realistic.

Attachment – the holy grail of a relationship

Keep in mind that trying to feel the way you felt in the first couple of months for the rest of your lives is not practical. That is a primeval mating instinct that we were born with so that we would be attracted to each other, procreate and move on. However the next stage where you now are might have fewer fireworks but should provide you with the incomparable feeling of being loved for who you are. Creating and maintaining attachment is the secret to maintaining the healthy state of the relationship.

Making an effort (why)

How many times have you heard others, or maybe even said yourself, 'I woke up one day and I was living with a stranger'?

And how many times has that phrase been the first gong in the death march of the relationship? Call it boredom; call it the loss of love; the fact of the matter is that this situation is usually down to at least one party no longer making the effort that is needed to keep a relationship ticking over. Usually it hasn't been a conscious decision – 'I can't be bothered anymore, let the chips fall where they may'. It just sets in like damp or dry rot and once it sets in it is hell and all to get rid of it – and you'll always worry about it coming back. So that's why you make an effort – an ounce of prevention is worth a pound of cure.

Making an effort (how)

Remember the chemical reactions we talked about earlier? The oxy-whatsits and the neo-doodah? Here's the thing – once they set in they tend to grow. In other words getting into the habit of making an effort makes it second nature; which then makes it a routine; which then makes it less of a big deal. The attachment grows and the more attached you become to each other the more you feel the need to reach out and maintain the attachment.

1 **Touching**. Touch your partner frequently, and not necessarily in a sexual way. Oxytocin is sometimes called 'the cuddle chemical'.

2 **Listen to each other**. People feel valued when they're listened to.

3 **Make eye contact with each other**. Sounds simple but you would be surprised how sometimes we are having a conversation while reading the paper, ironing, or staring at the telly.

4 **Stop what you're doing and properly greet each other** at the end of the day.

5 **Hold hands when you're sleeping**.

6 Get in the habit of **doing new things together**.

7 **Date each other**. Once a month without fail go on a proper date. No kids. Nice clothes. Away from the house.

8 **Have dreams and goals and work towards them**. Doesn't matter how small they are. Saving £50 for a double massage session. Build a birdcage together. Doesn't matter what it is as long as it is something that you will dream together, plan together, and work on with each other.

9 **Compliment each other** regularly.

10 **Surprise each other with little things**. Tuck her favourite chocolate bar in her purse. Book him a test-drive in his dream car.

I know it all sounds like a lot of work but isn't your happiness worth it?

Spending time together

This tends to be more of an issue in relationships where children are involved. Your natural instinct might be to put your children first, and while they are your priority so is your relationship. You can do both – give your children what they need and keep the relationship between you and your partner alive. But it takes planning.

"Trouble is part of
your life and if you
don't share it you
don't give the person
who loves you
a chance to love
you enough."

Dinah Shore

The role of the clock in your relationship

With the best will in the world there are only 24 hours in a day. Work, children, day to day practicalities and by the time you're finished there's precious little time or energy left for your relationship. Yes you are both in the same boat but there are often gender differences as to how this situation is regarded. Women often feel 'We're both in the same situation' and assume that the man understands. Men often feel 'She's only interested in the children, what about me?' This is a serious dilemma and often when you sit down with a couple in crisis the lack of quality time spent together will often be cited as the reason behind the demise of the relationship.

Making time for the two of you

Without careful attention you run the risk of totally losing sight of each other. This is another reason why the suggestions in the *How to make an effort* section are so important. Keeping each other within easy reach is a lot easier than trying to reach across an abyss.

When my son was born someone told us that we should always take one holiday a year without him and it would go a long way towards keeping our love alive. We nodded politely and promptly laughed as soon as the person left the room. He was wealthy; he and his wife had household help – easy for him to say. But when you think about it most of us have a set of willing grandparents or aunties and uncles willing to look after your offspring for a week. Especially if you're willing to return the favour.

The holiday solution – don't knock it till you've tried it

We found that there were more benefits to be gained from taking a cheap one week holiday just the two of us, then a cheap one week holiday en famille. Believe it or not the cost is about the same as taking one fancy two week holiday and the benefits are incalculable. You have one week a year to rekindle whatever might need rekindling within yourself and between the both of you. You come back refreshed and invigorated. Go home drop off the bags with the bikinis and massage oil and pick up the kids, the bucket and spade and off you go. You'll find you enjoy the kids more when you're rested.

One minute a day that will save your relationship

Be it one minute a day or one week a year – give each other some Us Time – it isn't a luxury, it's a necessity.

Spotting trouble and nipping it in the bud

One of the most important habits you should get into is talking through issues as they come up. This does NOT mean nagging. It doesn't mean constantly finding fault or complaining. But it does mean having a proper non-parental, non-judgemental discussion when there is a problem. If something is important then ignoring it will not make it disappear. In fact usually ignoring it will just make it grow bigger and more difficult to deal with.

"A successful marriage requires falling in love many times, always with the same person.

Mignon McLaughlin

Don't stick your head in the sand

If you are paying attention to the state of your relationship you will usually be aware when something is not right. Please don't fall into the habit of calling your mother or your girlfriends 'Something's wrong with Alan what do you think it is?' If you want to know what's wrong with Alan then, errrrm, ask Alan. A simple 'Are you OK, you seem a bit distracted/quiet/sad/down lately, is there anything I can do?' – lets the person know that you have noticed that something is off and you're there if they want to talk. If the person's behaviour has changed radically then ask yourself 'Has she always done that and I've just never noticed it?' If you can definitely say that it is new behaviour and you're not comfortable with it then 'I notice that you've been staying out with the people from the office a lot lately, is something wrong and would you like to talk about it?'

Solving problems

There are times in even the best of relationships when you come upon stumbling blocks. It could be anything from, you want a conservatory and he wants a new sports car, to she doesn't want to have another child and you do. While how you communicate can be the make or break factor in your relationship, so can how you problem-solve. Because of this it is good to have a problem-solving strategy in place and use it for anything from 'I want to change the wallpaper' to 'Should we move to Newcastle?'

1 **Identify the problem**. If the problem is a big one usually that won't take too much effort but sometimes the problem is 'just a feeling' in which case you might need to sit down and give it some thought.

2   **Create some possible solutions**. Give some thought to one or two possible solutions, in other words, don't come to the table empty-handed. You want to solve the problem together not just dump it on the other person.

3   **Construct a proper time to sit down and talk about it**. I cannot repeat enough times that it is often not what you've said but how and when you say it that determines whether or not you have a successful outcome.

4   **Get their opinion on the situation**. How many times have I heard 'Well she didn't really care what I thought, she had it all worked out so I didn't even bother to comment'? At each step of the way ask their opinion. Step One: 'I've been thinking about x, y, z and the more I think about it is the more I realise what a big problem it is. Do you agree?' Step Two: 'I don't know how we could go about solving it, I was thinking maybe we could try a, or b but I'm not sure. What do you think of those ideas or do you have any ideas that you think might work better?'

If solving the problem is going to involve investigating certain possibilities then suggest that you do it together, 'Let's go on the Internet and see what we can find', 'How about we make an appointment at the bank for next week and go in and speak to someone?' Sharing the responsibility for solving big problems is one of the most important building blocks of a successful relationship.

Keeping up appearances

This section should really be called 'elbows off the table, track-suit bottoms in the bin'. When you talk to women about the state of their relationship they will often cite the change in their partner's behaviour as cause for concern. When you talk to men about the state of their relationship they will often cite the state of their partner's appearance as their cause for concern. Yes sometimes the appearance or behaviour has definitely changed, but quite often if we're honest with ourselves we've just stopped making the effort. It's easier to haul on the tracksuit bottoms to do the school run or when you come in from a hard day in the office.

Guys you know she loves you so leaving the loo seat up or commenting loudly on bodily functions should be one of the benefits of settledom should it not? Well not really. There is no need for her to look like Bagpuss's Granny or you to behave like Rab C.Nesbitt on a bender — or vice versa of course. So try to make a bit of effort, both of you, you'll feel all the better for it.

The role of romance

Let's start this topic by clearing up two of the most widely held misconceptions. Ladies — romance is not only something that boys do for girls — enjoying romance is not gender specific. Gentlemen — romance is not necessarily expensive and is definitely not always a precursor to sexual activity.

Women are always complaining to me that their men are not romantic. Then I ask 'When was the last time you did something romantic for him?' I get a blank look and sometimes even a 'We don't have to do it for them they're supposed to do it for us!' Oh really? I must have missed that page in the rule book then.

And boys why is it that when your women ask you do something romantic you so often choose Option **A** – flowers from the petrol station, or Option **B** – something involving red lace fingerless gloves.

We both like it, we both need it

OK both of you listen up. True Romance is equally important to both sexes and whilst it often leads to sex it doesn't have to. In ancient times marriages were usually arranged and were primarily business relationships based on property, money, or political alliances. Then in medieval times the importance of romance in relationship to marriage came into the picture so that troubadours and poets could run a brisk trade in soppy songs and poems. It's been downhill ever since.

How to be romantic (even if you've never been before)

Do you want to know what the secret to romance is? **Romance is something that you do or say to your loved one that no one else could do or say and have the same meaning**. Here's an example. You buy her a giant diamond ring from Tiffany's that's *very nice*. You buy her the same diamond ring and bury it in a can of baked beans because that was the first thing she ever cooked for you – ***that is romantic***. You can buy her the latest bottle of designer perfume or you can make her a compilation CD of her favourite songs. You can rent his favourite DVD (even if it is *Die Hard 17*), cook his favourite meal (even if it's Polish sausage and trifle) ***that is romantic***. And when they say 'You remembered................' you know you have a result!

"Tis the most
tender part of love,
each other to forgive.

John Sheffield

Talking about s-e-x

In our current climate, where 5-year-olds are being taught about the birds and the bees and we know the intimate details of our newsreaders' sex lives, it is difficult to believe that we still have difficulties talking about sex. Why is that you might wonder. When our grandparents were younger sex was a very private matter. You might be aware that you weren't being satisfied. You might wish that the person on top (or underneath) you didn't just lie there thinking of England – but you certainly weren't going to say anything. You might know something was missing but you could only guess what it was.

Why you must talk if there is a problem

Nowadays everywhere you turn there is an article telling you exactly and with great detail what should be happening to you. Billboards and telly adverts will show you the wonderful sexual experiences you are missing if you're not using the right dandruff shampoo or driving the right car. You might think that this constant exposure and over-familiarisation with matters sexual would make it easy for us to discuss, but for most of it hasn't. In fact for a fair few of us it is even more difficult. But if it is an issue in your relationship then discuss it you must.

Starting the conversation

Sex within a relationship is a very sensitive subject indeed and needs to be approached carefully. Some people seem to find it easier to tell a total stranger 'I prefer when you do it *this* way' than to say the same thing to someone with whom they are in a committed relationship. You may be worrying that you might hurt their feelings, you might just not know how to say it, you might be shy but here are some tips. Compliment the current state of play 'I love the way it feels when you do that' (if you're brave you can say what 'that' entails). Then follow that by 'Is there anything special you would like me to do?' If there is a particular move that your partner thinks makes them the king or queen of the bedroom and it makes you want to run screeching then a simple 'You know I love it when you do x but I am kind of less fond of y. Is there anything I do that you'd prefer I didn't do?' At the end of the experience 'I really did enjoy that'.

Getting wild if you want to

If your issues involve wanting to broaden your horizons go to the nearest bookstore and look through the shelves. There are dozens of books that you and partner can go through together, in fact consider making a night of it. Go to the bookstore, choose a book or two, have a bottle of wine chilling then go home and see what comes up.

Caught red-handed

It isn't my job to wax eloquent on the level of morality you should display if you are trying to keep your relationship healthy; commonsense should tell you to behave yourself. But we're not all angels and there are few relationships out there that don't have one or two rainy days often centring around someone getting caught out. That could mean anything from spending half the household budget on shoes to sleeping with someone's sibling.

Now here's an interesting thing that I have gleaned from my years of agony aunting and counselling folk. Men tend to get caught, women don't. I'll give you a couple of minutes to digest that...

Bad behaviour gender differences

If a man finds himself in an untenable situation he will often behave badly in an attempt to get you to 'relieve him of his responsibilities'. Many times when a man starts playing away from home or exhibiting one or another sort of inappropriate behaviour it is the proverbial cry for help or cry for freedom. With women, usually whatever the misbehaviour entails is either something they *really* want to do (like buy the shoes), or they have convinced themselves that they are deeply in love with someone but feel their familial responsibilities are too precious to abandon. So whatever they do they plan and execute it in such a way that discovery is not a necessary part of the situation.

Someone's been 'naughty'; someone is now **very** sorry!

1 **Be honest**. If you are confronted then admit to your misdemeanour. If you want to hold onto your relationship then you must attempt to wipe the slate clean. Lies on top of bad behaviour are never a good idea.

2 **Be brief**. The wronged party might demand a lot of detail; it is usually wise to discourage this. 'The shoes were only £250 and they're usually £500' is one thing; 'I did it because I thought he would be better in bed and he has a lot of money' is another.

3 **Allow the other person the space to vent their feelings** (as long as it is not physical – that is never acceptable). If there are children then the discussion needs to be had either away from the house or the children need to be shipped off somewhere. Please do not think that they're asleep so they won't hear, or they are too young and they

won't understand. I have worked with many traumatised adults now in their 30s and still wondering what made Mummy sleep with Uncle Bernie.

4 **Don't make promises you have no intention of keeping**.

5 **Say you're sorry and really mean it**. You may not regret whatever your action was but chances are you really are sorry to have hurt your loved one and you must say so.

Forgive and forget

Many moons ago some bright spark decided that the word Forgive needed to be permanently attached to the word Forget. Forgive 'n' Forget became the Fish 'n' Chips of the world of relationships, romantic or otherwise. So let's understand something right now.

Which is possible – which is not

It is possible, and relatively within the range of accomplishment to forgive. But the only thing one forgets are where you put the car keys and what day is her birthday again? This is a very, very important thing to know when involved in a long-term relationship, and the earlier in the relationship that you master the technique, the stronger your chances of survival and success. Here's the deal – first you forgive; which translates to 'deal with the information in a healthy fashion'. Then you put it away neatly.

Learning to forgive

Step 1. Try if possible to understand what happened and why.

Step 2. Let it be known that you were hurt/angry/saddened by what happened.

Step 3. Express your feelings about how you would react if the situation were to be repeated.

Step 4. Put it in a box up on a shelf.

Leave the sore tooth alone

Don't try to bury it or burn it; that gives it power to come back and haunt you. It follows the 'don't think about carrots' rule. You'll think about nothing but. Better you take away the power that the thought has then it is less likely to come back and haunt you. You know the tooth is sore, don't poke it.

How not to be haunted by bad memories

This technique is very difficult I am not going to tell you otherwise. It takes practice and faith that it will work and after a while, like most of the stuff we are talking about, it becomes a way of life. It took me about a year to get it right but I know some of you will be much cleverer than I at getting the hang of it. Once I got the hang of it I even went back and applied the technique to lots of old monsters that were lurking around in the nooks and crannies of my mind. Managed to clear out a whole lot of rubbish and felt all the better for it.

Why DIY is worth it

None of us are angels and though we live in an 'it's broken don't fix it just bin it' society, that's not really the way to go. It probably took quite a while to find this person and before you walk away you owe it to yourself to do whatever you can to make it work.

Pocket Primer – S.C.R.T.S. to a successful relationship

Sharing

Caring

Respect

Trust

Support

'Who knew it would be this difficult?' is what people now say after a half-hearted attempt is made at anything from a new diet, an exercise programme, or a relationship. Why do we no longer really try to make things work? Our Instant Gratification culture has us so brainwashed that if we don't immediately lose that half a stone, have the skin of a 9-year-old or the life of the fantasy couple of the moment then bin it. Whatever it is or whoever it is. We were the 'anything is possible generation' and now so many of us are the 'can't be bothered to make a proper effort' generation.

We want Instant Perfection in a can – and it doesn't exist. This is one of the reasons our divorce rate is what it is; and has a lot to do with why so many of us are miserable. Take a look around your life at your unread self-help books (we all have them). I have a house full of use-this-and-you-don't-need-to-go-to-the-gym gadgets. The operative words are 'use this' not 'keep it in the back of the cupboard and it will work miracles from there'. Bin a relationship too easily and you might find yourself looking back later in life when it's too late, realising that with a little bit of work it really would have been the one.

Every instance of heartbreak can teach us powerful lessons about creating the kind of love we really want.

Martha Beck

If love ends

chapter 4
If love ends

Any real relationship will have its peaks and valleys. The minute we see a dip in the flames of passion many of us will be convinced 'It's finished! When will I ever learn?' But a proper relationship is like a sapling that needs constant tending to grow into a mighty oak tree. However the day might come when you have done everything you can think of to save your relationship. It seems like you're trying to put out a forest fire with a teapot – yes you may indeed be in trouble. There have been sessions with a counsellor, a weekend in Paris – still nothing.

When you try to talk it through it seems as though you're repeatedly banging your head on the pavement. Your conversations never resolve anything and just go round and round and you end up feeling frustrated and confused. Any discussion lasting longer than a few minutes has the potential to end up in a shouting match. What else can one say?

Maybe it really is time to move on.

Just check, double-check and triple-check that you've tried everything because these days a good love is hard to find. If you make it through a rough patch you will often find your relationship stronger and greatly improved. Sometimes there will be a spectacular view you've not seen before right on the other side of the valley you're currently in.

No way to go but out

There are basically two ways that a relationship ends; either with a big bang or a whimper.

BIG BANG – something happens that is too big to move beyond. You have discussed it, you've possibly forgiven or maybe you can't – whatever the reason you've come to the end of the road and wild horses couldn't keep you from packing your bags. Maybe your anger is at a level that you cannot return from or worse maybe you've frozen cold. Whatever the emotional temperature there is no light at the end of the tunnel full-stop.

WHIMPER – are you finding that together you laugh a lot less than you used to? Has the frequency and quality of your sex life changed dramatically? Do you find yourself arguing more and listening less? Are you less interested in each other's lives? Do you spend more time daydreaming about the good times past than enjoying any good times present? Think about the two of you five years from now. What do you see and how does it make you feel?

One last thing before you leave

I would be remiss in my duties if I didn't give you a bit of advice. Whether or not you want to hear it probably depends on whether you regard the demise of your relationship as Big Bang or Whimper.

Before you end it why not try to get an impartial observer to take a look at the situation and see if there is anything that can be done to save the relationship. There are as many different types of help as there are relationships. There are relationship counsellors. Agony aunts. If you're religious you can go to your vicar, priest, imam, rabbi or whatever the head of your religious organisation is called. Whichever avenue you choose counselling basically has three stages.

Stage One: both parties get the opportunity to put forth their perception of the situation. What has happened to date and how you would like to see the situation change.

Stage Two: the counsellor/impartial observer will help clarify why these issues are causing difficulty to the relationship – without laying the blame at either door.

Stage Three: then he or she will help you both identify the pluses and minuses of your relationship and help you come up with possible strategies for repairing and strengthening the situation. While there is no guarantee that it will work, most people feel that it helps either the state of the relationship or dealing with the aftermath.

Making the decision

OK are you sure about this? Have you thought it through carefully? Is there a specific problem and if so have you tried to solve it? What are the ramifications of this break-up? Are there children involved, shared property etc? While it is human nature for most folk to want to discuss major events in their lives please be careful about how, who, when, and where you discuss this issue with others.

I have known of many instances of people who were only toying with the idea of ending a relationship, shared their thoughts with one too many people and lo and behold ended up having the decision made for them. Ending up on the wrong end of a 'I heard you were about to break it off with me so let me save you the trouble' kind of conversation is not a nice place to be.

Making a difficult decision easier

Before you get to the 'discussing it with all and sundry' stage there is something you might want to try. It is one of my personal favourite life tools and can be used in just about any kind of decision making process. It is called A Balance Sheet. Take a piece of A4 paper and divide it into two halves. Across the top of the left hand column write 'Pros' and across the top of the right hand column write 'Cons'. Then let your mind flow naturally. You will find it is like your pen has a mind of its own. Don't stop to think about what you're writing, how many you're writing or if you're sure you really want to write it down. No one but you will ever see this list (by the way that's an order not a request) and whether or not it does what it is supposed to will be totally dependent on your honesty and free hand. Allocate yourself at least 15 minutes for this and I tell you it will be 15 minutes well spent. Usually when you sit back and look at the paper in its entirety the answer to your question is clear as day.

Breaking up

You've realised that there was a problem. You've discussed it with your partner. You've been to counselling. You've done your Balance Sheet and realised there were more Cons than Pros so it is the end and it must be said.

No texting. No emails. No cards. 'I never expected to find myself saying this, but I think it might be better if we went our separate ways. We have had a wonderful time together but for the past two years I have become more and more unhappy and if I am this unhappy, I suspect you are as well. We've both made an effort and tried to improve things, but I think this is as good as it's going to get and for me this isn't enough. We both deserve to be happier than we are now. I would like to hope, after all we've been through that we would wish only the best for each other'...

Two things to remember

There are two important things to keep in mind.

1 **This too shall pass**. As badly as you may now feel and as impossible as it may be to believe – you will not always feel the way you feel now. The sun will shine again, or the birds sing, or whatever passes for happiness in your world.

2 When something dreadful happens in your life **it is only a wasted experience if you learn nothing from it**. No matter how awful the situation there is always something to be gained. It could improve your approach to relationships and the way you live your life. Make sure you find some way to use what has transpired towards improving your future.

Dealing with practicalities

Whatever the length or intensity of the relationship there are going to be practicalities that need to be dealt with. Anything from who gets the James Blunt CD to who gets the dog. If you don't live under the same roof then gather together anything around the house that might belong to the other person. Let them know that you have their things ready for collection and if possible could they please gather anything of yours so you can arrange an exchange. If it is too painful then send a courier or enlist a kind friend. However upset you might be please don't throw all the stuff in a bin bag and resist the urge to cut the sleeves off his suits or anything similarly childish. It might bring temporary relief but in the long run you will most likely regret it.

If you have been living under the same roof then it gets hugely more complicated and there is a list of things that need to be attended to. (*Children will be dealt with in a separate section.)

1   Who is going to move out?

2   What is a reasonable amount of time in which this should be accomplished? If the situation is intolerable then one of you might move out temporarily and stay with a friend. Be sure to check the legalities of this before doing so as there are certain instances where moving out could affect your rights.

3   Make a schedule for moving out.

4   Make a list of any financial obligations that are shared or pertain to the property and determine how they are going to be handled.

5   Check schedules to see if there are any issues that need to be addressed like pre-booked holidays, family occasions etc. and decide how these situations should be dealt with.

6   Get all the papers together pertaining to things like mortgages, insurance, vehicle ownership etc. and go through them writing up a schedule for how they are going to be handled. Photocopy the papers so that you each have a file. If you are getting divorced then be sure to discuss all of the above and do not agree to anything without first discussing it with either your attorney or any of the organisations, such as Citizens Advice, that give support in these instances.

7   Set a timetable by which all the practicalities will be sorted out.

"Divorce is the psychological equivalent of a triple coronary by-pass. Following such a monumental assault on the heart, it takes years to amend all the habits that led up to it.

Mary Kay Blakely

Telling the world

Across the pond an entire industry has sprung up around notifying people about the demise of you relationship. With the usual Yank attitude of 'making the best of a bad situation' there are announcement cards, parties; there are even round-robin e-cards! However we tend to be more dignified on this side of the Atlantic so most of us will not be in a big rush to send out a card saying 'Husbands are like guns, keep one around long enough and you're gonna want to shoot it!'

Saving your emotional energy for the important things

At times like this the world can be divided into two halves – those who you want to tell because they will really care; and those who need to be told even though they're just nosey. I have to say that from experience I think you have enough to deal with without having to answer a lot of questions which are either painful or no one's business. Those people with whom you are genuinely close you will have a conversation with if and when you are ready. The rest of them can discuss it amongst themselves.

Spreading the word

It is now perfectly acceptable to send an email or do a change-of-address card: 'As of March 1st, 2008 Robert Williams originally of 3 Mandeville Road, London NW3 4YH, will be residing at 48 Twizzlehurst Lane, Marsh-upon-Thames, OX7 39. Any correspondence, business or personal, should be directed to that address. The mobile number remains the same'. This can be sent to anyone from utility companies to the GP and the people at the golf club; from close friends (you can write 'call me' on the bottom) to not-so-close friends. There is nothing worse than bumping into folk who don't yet know and having to tell them in the frozen food aisle at Tesco – trust me on that one.

Telling the family

Close family should not be on the 'change of address' list. And needless to say close family should be told before 'the world'. How this is handled depends on a couple of things: does your family live next door or in Spain? The circumstances of the situation, is it acrimonious or terribly civilised? I have known people who have invited both their families over and said 'There's something Bob and I want you to know...' I've known people who have written 'Dear Mom and Dad it is with great sadness that I write to tell you that it looks like Bob and I are going to go our separate ways'.

Putting into words

Personally I would say that if you can, you should sit down with a cup of tea and tell them in person. For the sake of your own emotional stability I suggest deciding in advance what you want to say 'I suspect it won't come as a surprise to you that as Bob and I have not been getting along very well over the past year we have now decided to call it a day'.

While you may want to be considerate to your family it is you and your state of mind that are important. Please don't be afraid to say 'If you don't mind I'd rather not talk about all the ins and outs. It's still all a bit raw and I need to keep it together for the children/work/the dog. I promise to give you all the gory details later, right now I just want to thank you for your support.'

Telling the children

As you can see I have saved the most important conversation for the last. There is nothing in the world more important than how you tell the children. You may bear the burden of losing your dreams but your children had no choice in the matter. Ending the relationship might have been your choice; it might lead to a better life, one in which you are happier. You have made an educated decision and your children will have to deal with it. If the children are pre-teen they will have little frame of reference for this sort of experience. They will probably have other children in their class whose parents are separated but when it happens to them it will almost certainly be the biggest thing in their life to date.

Breaking it gently

Whatever differences you and your partner may have, you need to pull together on this one. You may no longer be a couple but you will always be parents. Sit down together and decide beforehand what you are going to tell the children. 'We have something important to tell you. You've probably noticed that Dad and I haven't been getting on for awhile and we think it's better that we no longer live together. This doesn't affect our feelings for you, we still love you, it's just that our feelings for each other have changed'. *It is also crucial that your children understand that this is in no way their fault!* 'We want you to know that this decision has nothing to do with how you kids behave. I know we occasionally squabble with you, but we couldn't possibly wish for a more wonderful group of children. This is **totally** about issues between Dad and I, do you understand?' (*See Pocket Primer for more tips.)

Giving your children a secure future

Parents separating no longer guarantees a life of ruin for a child. Thank heavens we've moved on a bit — BUT it does have to be handled very carefully. First you need to keep in mind that subconsciously children consider themselves to be a combination of both their parents. What this means is that when you speak badly about your ex the part of your child that corresponds with that parent will feel badly. And if when your child is with your ex that parent speaks badly about you then the other half of the child will respond emotionally to that. In other words they will take it personally. If you put together two sad halves then you will end up with one sad whole and I'm sure you don't want that.

Bad-mouthing your ex can destroy your kids

Most of the time parents will swear up and down 'I never ever say anything bad to the children about their mother/father. Oh no I would never do that!' Then you speak to the children and find out that while they may not direct the comments to the children they will have conversations with all and sundry where the children are in earshot and the effect is the same.

I have had more children tell me 'Mummy always talks about Dad on the phone to Grandma and what she says really upsets me...' than I've had hot dinners. And of course as you think the children can't hear the conversations, that's when the inappropriate-for-a-child's-ears information comes tumbling out. So if you don't want to answer questions like 'How come you're going to slap Daddy's secretary' or 'How come Daddy punched Uncle Steve in the eye' then keep your conversations for when there is absolutely no chance of being heard.

What children care about most

The other important thing that will help your child feel as secure as possible is attention to practicalities. Children are basic creatures. They are not uncaring but quite possibly, no matter what their age, they have not yet developed a level of emotional intelligence that will enable them to absorb the ramifications of what is happening. Children however do understand their needs and their first worries will often be based around what they know and understand. 'Will we have to move?' 'Do I have to go to a different school?' 'Where will Dad live?' 'When will I see Dad?' 'Will we still go to Spain in July?' 'Will Dad still take me to football?' 'Will we still get to see Granny and Grandad?' It might seem at the time that they don't care or understand – they do care and they understand as much as they can. What they are doing is instinctively checking what in their world is still 'safe'. That is why it is important that you gather all this information together before you have the big conversation.

Simple phrases to help keep them in balance

Go straight from the phrases in the section from above into the 'Now don't worry you won't have to move, you'll stay at your school. Your Dad is going to be living ten minutes away and you'll see him............etc. etc.'

How to move on from this difficult conversation

End the conversation with 'We know this is a lot for you to take on board so we thought maybe we could sit down again tomorrow in case you think of anything else you might want to ask.

And of course if you want to talk before then just let us know'. When we had to have this conversation with our son (he was ten) I also gave him a piece of paper the next day with five telephone numbers on it. They were his godfather, his godmother, his paternal grandparents, my mother, and a close family friend. I told him that I understood that he might want to talk about it and feel uncomfortable discussing it with either of us so he was to feel free at any time to call any of them. Three years later and he did take advantage of two of the numbers. My ex and I decided a year and a half ago to take him to a child psychologist for a bit of a road test. He was being so incredibly calm and well-adjusted that we thought he might be burying his true feelings. The psychologist told me afterwards that he really and truly was completely fine. She said that whatever we had done I should write a book about it, so here we are. ☺ It might still be early days; and if there had been any other way I would have wanted my marriage to continue. But sometimes life gives you lemons and then you just need to make lemonade.

You are still a family

This is a very tricky one and how it is handled will usually depend on the nature of the break-up and the personalities of the people involved. But let me say again – **it's about the children**. If there are no kids involved you can wave goodbye to your ex and never ever see them again for as long as you both shall walk this earth. But if there are children, that is a luxury you will not have.

Making the rest of your lives easier

There is nothing that breaks my heart more than people asking my advice on what to do because they are about to get married and the one blot on the landscape is that one or other parent is refusing to come because of the possible attendance of the other parent. I have seen this happen time and time again and often when you ask how long ago the separation occurred you will find 'oh they split up when I was eleven'. For heaven's sake don't find yourself in that sort of situation, don't do that to your kids – let it go.

It is going to be torturous in the beginning. For the first year after my marriage ended it was all I could do to be in the same room with him. But religiously I battled on. Ten days after he left it was our son's tenth birthday and we went to Brighton for the day – possibly the worst day of my life and it was on the train on the way back that I quietly removed my wedding ring. Then came the first Christmas and I invited him to the house for Christmas lunch. I spent half the day running back to what used to be the marital bedroom, crying my eyes out, composing myself and coming back out.

How did I survive or why did I do it? Because the light at the end of the tunnel was the hope that by doing it I could in some small way give my son something that he had inadvertently been robbed of.

Sharing the duties of parenting

How is it now? Three years down the road most weeks we might have a meal together, Saturday lunch after music school. We go to school meetings together. The school has both of us listed as primary contacts. Homework duties are shared, as are punishments and big decisions. The result of 'being civilised' is that you have a situation where **your child feels part of a family even though you are not still part of a couple**. You will also find that encouraging this kind of atmosphere will make it easier when either of you introduces a new partner.

Being clear about your status

You must also be certain that you have clearly set out the boundaries to explain that though you all spend time together that you are NOT getting back together as a couple – you must be very clear about that.

Being civil

This is a bit of a hodgepodge topic but if I had to boil it down to two sentences it would be **Don't make a show of yourself** and/or **To live well now** – **_that_ is the best revenge**.

Let's address the first one. Dignity – it's all about maintaining it at all costs. I know you're angry right now, maybe the red mist has even settled in but you really don't want to look back on this period of time with shame. How to avoid going down the wrong road? Try to avoid 'drowning your sorrows' – that's usually the fastest road to trouble. If there is someone else involved in the situation try to avoid ALL contact with that person. Your relationship was with your ex and if there is blame to be apportioned it should be with the person you were in a relationship with, not some stranger. This means no raving loony messages into anyone's answering machine at 2 am – not your ex's not the new person's. It also means no telling all your friends 'He was rubbish in bed', 'She's lying, those are not real'; you just look childish. Think 'Rise above it' and 'I won't stoop to his/her level' – write it on your sleeve, post it on your mirror, make it your screensaver – do whatever you have to do but live it, you'll feel all the better for it.

Alternatives to revenge

Now let's move on to the other self-esteem wrecker: **Revenge** – some say it is a dish best served cold, some say revenge is sweet. I'd say it's a dish best not served at all and is a sour taste indeed. I've been there, been so mad I thought I'd never be able to breathe again until I throttled someone and of course I knew who I wanted that person to be. But don't do it. Yes, release your anger – beat pillows, write letters that you're never going to post. Go to the beach and scream until you're hoarse, but then go home with your head held high and get on with your life. As the saying goes, live your life well – as if you're 'just not bovvered' – and one day you really won't be.

Chapter summary:

Pocket Primer – Telling the children

1. Keep it simple.

2. Explain the practicalities.

3. Schedule when they will see the departing parent.

4. Identify the things in their lives that will remain the same.

5. Leave the door open for continuing the conversation.

The relationship has ended. You had a dream, possibly one that you've had for a very long time and now it's disappeared, and probably not quietly. For one reason or another your world as you know it has totally altered. No matter how much you may wish it, nothing will ever be the same again. You would have gone into this situation with the best of intentions, you worked as hard as you could in the best of faith but it didn't work. You are not a failure, you are not a victim, sadly it didn't work out but you'll pick yourself up and carry on. You'll learn whatever lessons need to be learned and start walking through the tunnel. You probably can't see the light at the end of it right now but it's there so, as the song says, 'pick yourself up and get back in the race...' This is life.

I love my past,
I love my present.
I'm not ashamed
of what I've had,
and I'm not sad
because I have
it no longer…

Colette

Starting over

chapter 5
Starting over

'Watching you walk out of my life does not make me bitter or cynical about love. But rather makes me realise that if I wanted so much to be with the wrong person then how beautiful it will be when the right one comes along.'
Anon

A lot of people nowadays (even the men) are asking – 'What do I do now?' 'What is the most important thing I need to know to start over?' Try as I might I cannot narrow it down to one invaluable bit of information. There are a few and I am going to share them with you, but let us begin with keeping this one thing in mind – it's never too late.

I've seen people fall head over heels in love in their 40s, 50s, 60s even 70s. So let's dust off the seat of our pants, get up slowly and hobble back towards the starting line – yes *again*! But I promise to make it easier this time.

Picking yourself up off the floor

I don't know about the rest of you but to me there are few things that feel worse than the end of a relationship. There can be a heck of a lot of pain in the ending of a three month relationship. As for the end of a 13 year marriage; I remember lying on a bed in a darkened room with my eyes closed thinking that if maybe I just held my breath long enough...

Taking the first steps

But you do have to 'just pick yourself up and get back in the race, because that's life...' How you deal with your break-up will largely be determined by your circumstances. If you are on your own then you can have tubs of ice cream and weepy DVDs. Or maybe you're an 'out on the town with your mates' kind of person. But if you have children your options become severely limited – I'm not sure if that's a good or bad thing.

On one hand it keeps you from putting a tea-cosy on your head and running around the garden naked screaming (or it should). And having to put out the fish fingers and beans of an evening will (hopefully) keep you from downing a bottle of Jack Daniels every night.

Releasing your emotions without frightening the livestock

However you do have to be careful that while you don't want to scare the children you do need to safely release your emotions. I think that a period of weeping, wailing and general gnashing of teeth is a good thing, perhaps even a necessity. But then the day comes when you find yourself noticing a bit of sunshine outside the window, or maybe you find yourself singing. Whatever it is, you can take it as a signal that it is high time you picked yourself up off the floor.

You are not a failure

Some people go into any new relationship with what I call the 'one foot out the door before you've even gone in' attitude. This relationship may or may not work and if it doesn't, oh well. There are a few things wrong with this kind of attitude the main one being that if you don't commit to success there is very little chance you will achieve it. And of course the old 'you get what you focus on' again comes into play so if you don't think it will work then there's a good chance it won't. The one advantage to having this kind of outlook is that when it all goes pear-shaped it is less of a shock to the system.

The one thing you must always remember

However if you're someone who goes into each new relationship with the 'this is forever and ever and ever' attitude, the realisation that this isn't so can be devastating. What we want to do here is to ensure, as best we can, that the damage is not permanent.

There are a couple of Big Concepts that we need to work through to make sure we clear out the mess properly. One, **you are not a failure**. Your relationship might have broken down. It might have failed. It might even have been down to you but you are not a failure. Yes I know I am repeating this 'you are not a failure' mantra but repetition is the mother of knowledge.

The role of the dream

What is a dream? A vision, an aspiration; something you are hoping for? An ambition you expect to achieve or a deeply held desire? However you define it at this particular moment in time you've lost your dream. Losing a dream is almost like experiencing a death. You are grieving for the loss of the person and the demise of a whole collection of hopes and aspirations.

Ask yourself this

There is a major turning point that you need to reach at the end of a break-up before you can start all over again and it's all about the dream. Ask yourself *what are you most bothered by* – the fact that this person is no longer in your life OR the fact that you've lost the dream.

The turning point

Please don't answer too quickly, this is a really big thought and it holds the key to your future. The moment that you realise, or begin to feel that it is less the loss of the person and more the loss of the dream is the moment you will begin to move forward. You might know it immediately or it might take you say.... 1 year, 7 months, 2 weeks, 3 days. 😊 But whenever it happens is when you'll know you're going to be ok. In the meantime there are some things we can do to jumpstart the process.

Changing the dream

The next thing we now need to do is change the dream. One of the most important rules in changing anything about your life is being willing to change the plan. If you're doing something and it isn't working then change it. And if the new thing doesn't work then change that as well. Tweak here, tweak there and eventually you will find the plan that accomplishes what you are striving for.

An aspect was wrong – not the entire concept

It is the same thing with relationships. You had a dream; you and Emma or Tarquin were going to spend the rest of your life together and live happily ever after – and it didn't work. You tried to fix it but it just didn't work and the dream collapsed. First we have to understand that it was that particular dream that fell apart. Not the dream of you ever finding happiness within a relationship – just the dream of you finding happiness in that particular relationship.

The secret to moving on successfully

So what do we do now? We change the dream. This doesn't mean immediately find a replacement for Emma or Tarquin and try to slot them into the same dream – it means **change the dream**. Or more accurately *create a space for a different dream which will hopefully become your new reality*. This means putting an end to endlessly bemoaning 'what could have been'. It's not going to happen, it's behind you...next!

Setting your new parameters

The one thing I would suggest doing before moving on however is to make yourself a small list. Write down all the things that did not work in your last relationship, try not to make it personal. 'Emma was really messy' isn't helpful. 'I am hoping for a tidy house now' is. In other words by listing the things that didn't work and changing them into positive statements for the future you are fine tuning your new dream.

Are you really ready?

I could tell you to put a post-it note up on your mirror with the words 'If at first you don't succeed try, try again' on it but trying again is what most of us do anyway. We suffer our first 'heart-break' in our teen years and once we learn the lesson that you won't really die from it we soldier on. Next Prince Charming or Perfect Girl comes around the corner and we're off at the races.

Then we usually stumble again and the entire process repeats itself.

Doing a safety-check

It is really important that when you decide to go back out into the world you really are ready. The mistake that a lot of us make is jumping back in before time. Figuring out whether or not the time is right is a bit tricky. Half of us want to run back out the front door before we're ready; the other half (if left to their own devices) would never go out the front door again. Why is this? And what separates us?

What happens if you go back too soon

The half that wants to run right back out are often of the mind that if they quickly 'fall in love' again that will erase the pain of the current bust-up. They will swear on their pet pig's head that it isn't what they're trying to do – but it is. Cries of 'Oh I'm not bovvered, I'm fine' usually mean 'uh-oh this one needs a bit more time'.

On the other side of the divide reside the people who very much felt every single drop of their pain and the idea of putting themselves in a position to possibly feel that awful again; well they just can't bear the thought of it. How do you know when you're ready? I would say halfway down the road from 'I'm not bovvered' and 'I think I'll just sit here in the dark a wee bit longer'. You probably won't just wake up one day and decide – 'ok I'm 100% fighting fit now'. And most likely whenever you decide, there might be a bit of nervous agitation at the thought but that's only normal.

1 Do you still find yourself thinking about the person a dozen or more times a day?

2 Do you still feel uncontrollable anger over the end of your relationship?

3 Or sadness?

4 Are you still to be heard declaiming loudly to anyone within earshot 'You do realise that all men/women are *&!!*+^s don't you?'

5 On a scale of 1-10 how would you rate your general state of mind?

If you answer yes to 2 of the first 4 and your answer to number 5 is under 6.5 then you're still not ready.

But let's skip ahead to some of the other tips so you can get yourself up to at least an 8!

How and why – not to become bitter

When a relationship ends it is difficult not to feel resentful, embittered, cheated or hard done-by. Some of us will also feel cynical about love and wonder whether or not it ever really does work. The saddest of all are those of us who quickly become resigned to the 'fact' that standing in the shards of a shattered relationship is the only place we will ever be.

It is hard not to be bitter and to find a way to heal your pain but you must make the effort to stave off the bitterness and eventually time will take care of healing the pain.

"If you were going to die soon and had only one phone call you could make, who would you call and what would you say? And why are you waiting?"

Stephen Levine

Survival of the fittest

The secret to not becoming bitter is to think of yourself as a survivor rather than a victim. Why do you think it is that decades later the opening strains of Gloria Gaynor's *I Will Survive* has us all running to the dance floor arms flailing wildly above our heads? And who amongst us doesn't know all the words? That's because that is what we are all looking for – the strength to live to tell the tale. We don't want to be a casualty of a failed relationship. Nor do we want to spend the rest of our life as walking-wounded; we want to rise like a phoenix from the ashes. We don't want to just survive, we want to triumph; and the first step towards achieving that is to permanently delete certain phrases from our vocabulary. **Victim Statement** – '*I can't believe he/she did that to me*'. **Survivor Statement** – '*I can't believe that whole thing happened but now I'll move on*'. I am not saying delete all knowledge of what has happened but stop thinking and speaking like a victim so you can change the bad memory into a positive hope and become a survivor.

Shedding the black cloud

Call it your aura, the atmosphere that surrounds you, your vibe, your mood – you can be certain that most people can figure out what kind of mood you're in without asking. It is also pretty much a rule that the more intense your mood the more 'visible' it is. You walk down the street very happy and you'll find strangers smiling at the sight of you. Sit on the bus dejected and down and if I'm sitting next to you I will burst out crying because I can feel your pain. I won't know what is wrong with you but I'll know that whatever it is you are really hurting. Here's something I've observed over the years – women tend to think they can hide their mood. They usually can't. Conversely, and most strangely, a man who cannot tell you where his other foot of sock is can spot a woman who is under a black cloud from a mile off. And no they don't have to be very intelligent men, or very sensitive men or any such thing. However most often they're single men. I don't know if it is a self-preservation technique but I am constantly amazed at how men can look at a woman walking down the street, turn to each other and say 'needy nutter' without exchanging a word. Then they get married and somehow some of them shed the capability to read their beloved's signals at 100 paces. 😊

Making sure the black cloud is gone

Anyway the point, is if/when you decide (be you male or female) to re-enter the world of relationships and dating you need to be sure that your black cloud has blown away. If not you're pretty much wasting your time. If you want to attract a happy, sane, well-adjusted person then you're going to need to look like a happy, sane, well-adjusted person as well. The danger about going out under the black cloud is that you will often attract someone who on a certain level is in the exact same space as you are. Needless to say two wounded birds do not a flying team make. I know it's hard to imagine getting out from under it, but it will happen. Don't try to push the cloud away. I promise it will gently flow away – but first you must let go.

Putting your baggage in the back of the shed

'Vengeance is having a videotape planted in your soul that cannot be turned off. It plays the painful scene over and over again inside your mind. And each time it plays you feel the clap

of pain again. Forgiving turns off the videotape of pained
memory. Forgiving sets you free.'
Lewis B. Smedes.

I don't remember exactly when it was that the term 'baggage' went from being a bit of Samsonite to meaning 'the excess emotional detritus of your past that you insist on carrying around with you'. But now if someone's says 'Oh she's got a lot of baggage' you immediately think, oh dear that's going to be three hours at dinner hearing about what this one or that one did to her. We know *you* are not going to be doing that because by now you've already memorised the How Not To Be A Victim mantras.

But in case they haven't yet sunken in here's a foolproof analogy. You know those little red wagons that kids drag around behind them with their toys, teddy bear and the raggedy blanket they wee on and won't let you wash? Well we as adults have them as well.

Why you must dump your baggage

If you ask the average woman who was the first man who broke her heart she will tell you his name was Calvin Claptrap, he was 9, he had a dog named Boo and he used to wear a stripey jumper every Tuesday. She will then be able to list every single man who did her wrong and produce detailed records of the circumstances. And if she digs around under the teddybear and the raggedy wee'd on blanket, she might even find a teaspoon full of pain as well. After awhile of doing this the first red wagon gets full and so she'll tie a second one on. Soon that one is full so she'll add a third and a fourth. Before you know it she is having trouble walking up the hill of life because she's dragging this unwieldy cavalcade behind her. Ask the average man the name of the first woman who broke his heart and he'll remember her name, he was usually about 19 and then after that he has nothing in his red wagon until you. I've met men who have to stop and think to remember the names of ex-wives! I could go into all sorts of anthropological reasons for why we're all the way that we are but that's not too much use right here and now so I won't. But what I will do is tell you that in life—ALL areas of life—**success goes to the light of baggage**.

Sorting what little to keep

If it isn't that important – fling it over the side (it's biodegradable). If it is that important then pick off all the meat, pack the bones in a box; and put the lot in the back of the shed behind the Christmas decorations and the old baby clothes. You don't need it and you'll move faster without it.

A shiny and new external you

One of the things that really gets my goat is this idea that your-life-is-falling-apart-but-here's-a-new-shade-of-lipstick-that-will-make-it-all-ok culture that we now live in. It drives me crazy, and it makes me sad. If you put frosting on a cowpat it is still going to smell like a cowpat, taste like a cowpat and be a cowpat. If you are down, depressed, angry and whatever other emotions you are struggling under the weight of, a new frock and some highlights is not going to make it all ok.

Treat yourself but don't go overboard

HOWEVER...having said all that, it can help and no I am not contradicting myself. What I am against is the thought that putting up lovely new wallpaper will miraculously repair the gaping cracks underneath. I have seen too many people do that and pay the price. Men buying big fancy cars, women buying Jimmy Choos. Come the end of the day you'll either be riding around in a big car still mad and on your own; or tottering along in a pair of stilettos still sad and on your own. A little bit of sprucing up will certainly lift your mood so feel free to indulge. Just make sure you realise that it might just be a case of hanging new curtains, there is probably still a bit of repair work to be done to get you fighting fit again.

An almost new and improved you (internal)

The temptation, especially if you feel you're the wronged party, is to demand an explanation either from the other person, or the other person's friends, family, or anyone who knew the both of you. 'What do you think went wrong?' 'Did he say anything to you?' – My attitude is slightly different from most on this subject (no surprise there). I think there is not much good to be gained from that line of thought or questioning.

Don't ask questions you don't really need answers to

'Is there anything you'd like to tell me?' or 'Well I'm sorry it didn't work out for us why do you think that was?' is, in my opinion, as far as questioning should go. There is a really good chance that you're not going to be told the truth. And frankly whatever you're told is not going to change the real problem which is that you're not going to be together anymore. Also it is quite subjective. 'I don't want to be with you anymore because you're too needy'. Well maybe you are but maybe you're not. So you're then going to walk around for the rest of your life thinking that you'll never have a proper relationship because you're too needy and it may not even be so. You would be surprised/horrified at some of the 'excuses' people will throw at you when backed into a corner. I once knew a man who broke off an engagement 'because she never had mayonnaise in the fridge!' I kid you not that is what he said and she dragged that around in her little red wagon for years after.

Learn how to be your own mirror

There is a phrase bandied about a lot these days, it is called being 'self-aware'. Basically translates to being aware of what is going on with you to an extent that you know yourself, thereby removing the need for you to be constantly searching for your reflection in mirrors held up by the outside world.

When you ask someone with whom you've just ended a relationship what was wrong with you and why they don't want to be with you any more, chances are you're holding yourself up in front a dirty, cracked, broken mirror and what you're going to have reflected back at you isn't going to let you know what you really look like.

Understanding what happened

One of the best things you can do for yourself whenever possible is to try to understand, for as much as this is possible, exactly what happened. As the saying goes if you don't understand your history you are destined to repeat it. This is a very difficult exercise because it will call for you to take a hard long look at yourself and right now frankly you might not have the strength for that. But if ever there was a good time for a little DIY self-improvement then this is it.

Kickstart the healing process

Find something small that you have wanted to work on for awhile, a new exercise regime, learning a new language, taking a philosophy class or taking up Tai Chi. Read a book you've been putting off – anything that will give you a sense of accomplishment. That is what you need to do now, feel good on the inside. Honestly it does all shine from within and we want to repair any cracks, shed that baggage, ban that dark cloud from over you, all the things we've said so far. So clean the windows of your soul and the light will shine through – sounds a bit hokey but it is oh so true.

What has changed since you last dated

Everything and nothing. The basic principle is still the same. Two people feel a possible attraction and think that spending some time together might be an enjoyable thing. The attraction might be purely physical, it might be intellectual, spiritual, shared morals or political beliefs or you made each other laugh on Facebook. Whatever it is the bottom line is you want to get to know this person better in some way and the best way to accomplish this is by spending more time together.

What's new if you haven't dated in five years

So what has changed? Well it depends on how long it's been. **If it's under five years** then probably nothing. Between five and ten years the ways of meeting people have really expanded. You will notice that many of the people you know (whatever your age or background) will be dating people they met on the Internet. They will either have met them on a dating site or some sort of discussion forum discussing anything from Tory politics to who is better Kaiser Chiefs or Radiohead (bands for the merrily uncool among us). You may also know people who have met on social networking sites like Facebook. (*If you go back to the first chapter on dating you will see some of the more popular methods we are now using to meet people.)

What's new if you haven't dated in ten years

If it has been **over ten years** you may find it surprising how much more competition there is. There seem to be fewer men and more women out on the circuit. There are possibly more openly gay men now and as most women are getting into committed relationships at a much later date the numbers are a bit unbalanced.

If it is over ten years since you last dated you may also be surprised at the number of women who now think absolutely nothing of asking a man out on a date. It has become de rigeur – if you've never done it it might take some getting used to. 'I was wondering if maybe you'd like to go out for a cup of coffee sometime' is easy and perfectly acceptable, especially for a newbie. If you find that quite difficult the old 'A group of us are going to (?) do you fancy coming along?' is really easy. It doesn't feel like you're asking them on a date and you will be less afraid of rejection.

> "Whenever I date a guy, I think, is this the man I want my children to spend their weekends with?"

Rita Rudner

What's new if you haven't dated in over fifteen years

If it's been **15 years or more** it might take a while for you to get used to one or two things that may or may not have been this way when you were last dating. The distance between saying hello and 'do you have condoms in your handbag?' might be appreciably shorter than you're used to. Do what makes you feel comfortable – if it makes you feel uncomfortable or pressured then don't. And nowadays women carry their own condoms – yes I know that does take a bit of getting used to as well. Bad enough we have to stroll through Boots with a carton of tampons we now have to slap down a multipack of condoms at the checkout.

You may also notice a lot more social mobility, less attention being paid to class. You may also notice more intra-religious dating than might have been around before. When you were last out a Church of England girl and a Catholic boy might have raised an eyebrow but now you wouldn't be surprised to see the vicar's daughter with a Buddhist or a Muslim. And of course the Baptist girl who is dating the ex-Hari Krishna.

What's new if electricity has been invented since the last time you dated

Last, but definitely not least, especially to those of us who have been off the scene for way over a decade, feel free to date whatever age you want to. Many of the women I know who are in their late 40s are dating men who are in their early to mid-30s. No money is changing hands, and there is nothing untoward about it. As we get younger at heart, fitter, happier, more independent, the range of people we attract broadens. Many of the men I know in the younger age ranges prefer older women, finding them more relaxed and comfortable in their skin. So if someone younger asks you out throw caution to the wind – you don't need it any more. Needless to say you don't have to run out and find yourself someone to break every social barrier you may ever have been conditioned into – just know that you're pretty much responsible to yourself now so do as you wish. However the cardinal rule is still the same 'choose wisely and carefully'...

What has not changed

Everyone wants to have a good time on a date. No one wants to be stressed out and pressured. Everyone wants to feel attractive and interesting. No one wants to be made to feel boring or not worth the effort. No one wants to feel you're only out with them because they will spend a lot of money on you. Neither does anyone want to feel they're being used for one thing or another. And of course most of us don't want to feel that sex is the only reason you're there. However a decade or so ago we would have been able to split this list neatly down the middle based on gender but no more. You're just as likely to find a man complaining 'she only wanted to sleep with me' and a woman saying 'I was so stressed out from work I just wanted to go home and go to sleep'. Yes there is still *Vive la difference* but now the difference will depend on the individual's personality rather than their gender, and that has made the whole enterprise much more fun.

Regaining confidence in the bedroom

Women: For many of us this is the toughest hurdle of all. I've had women sitting across from me with tears streaming down their face at the very thought of taking off their clothes in front of someone new. They've been disrobing in front of only one person for a whole lot of years without thinking about it, now it's back to Square One.

Taking advantage of the tricks of the trade

Here's the good news. There is now an entire industry based around showing women how to make the best of whatever they've got. There are about 45 different types of undergarments guaranteed to cure whatever evil befalls you. There are creams, potions, lotions to make sure you have the skin of a new born yak. You can revitalise your hair, whiten your teeth, you name it and you can do it. But you know what is the most important thing of all? – It's self belief.

Belief is the key to success

For anyone else to think you are attractive and sexy you've got to believe it yourself, and *really believe it.* I know you've probably heard this before but I am here to tell it to you again because it is the only truth. I've seen women tarted up to the nines who don't believe in themselves and they could be invisible for the amount of attention they're getting. And then I've seen women not nearly as attractive in the conventional sense but they feel good about themselves and people respond to that.

For many of us by the time we're out there on the market a second or third time, we're not 'selling' our possible capabilities as baby makers. It's about who we are, the lessons we've learned, the patina of experience that glows off us – that's what makes us attractive and sexy.

Taking charge of who you are

Go take up Tai Chi, take some belly dancing lessons, check out Julie Peasgood's *The Greatest Sex Tips in the World* – get your mojo working again and it will all be alright on the night. Don't worry about **The First Time**. I have yet to hear of a man who upon a woman removing most of her clothing said 'eww' and ran out the door. One of the lovely things about most men is by the time they've got their shoes and socks off wild horses couldn't turn them back. ☺

Men: Jumping under the duvet with someone other than the warm pair of feet you've been used to for over a decade can be just as scary for men as women. Just as many men worry about their attractiveness and, even more scary, whether or not they will be able to perform. If I had 50p for every man who has cried into his soup about losing his hair (gentlemen – that bothers you it does not bother us) I would be in the South of France writing this book. And gentlemen, worrying about the fact that you are no longer capable of maintaining an erection for six hours or 'doing it' four times a night – well frankly most women I know don't care. Now if you're going to insist on going out with girls then I guess you might need to go see the GP and get some assistance. But if you're going for 'the more mature woman' we don't want you to do it several times a night – just make sure the one time you do it, you do it right. ☺

Doing it all over again

This is a different kind of 'doing it' than we discussed above. This is about the whole thing.

This is about taking the chance at love, companionship, whatever it is that you are looking for. Look, if you get sick eating a bad meal in a restaurant you may choose not to go back to that restaurant but you certainly don't take a decision never to eat out again. I know that might sound like an overly simplistic analogy but as my father used to say – keep it simple.

'Yes but what if I get hurt again?' – Fine, then you reread this book.

It's never too late

I recently met a couple in their 70s who came to me for a kind of MOT on their relationship. They met and married in their late 60s and both of them believe that for the first time in their life they are truly in love. They feel that every wrong turn gave them a lesson that they now can use to be committed, dedicated and strong in their relationship with each other. I watched them walk away from our meeting holding hands (having told them that in my humble opinion they were more than fine) and when she leaned over and rested her head on his shoulder I thought 'oh I'd like some of that'. Then when he reached over and patted her backside lovingly I thought 'YES!!!'

Chapter summary:

Pocket Primer – Getting back on the bike

1. You are never too tired/old/past-it to start over.

2. Your relationship might not have worked out, just means it wasn't as right as you originally may have thought. Now you're free to find the right one or allow it to find you.

3. Look at yourself and decide what your good points are. Focus on them and be proud of them. Do it quietly and you will find your self-confidence growing slowly but steadily.

4. Learn to be pleased and happy by yourself within yourself and others will naturally gravitate towards you.

5. Yes you don't have to be with someone, but it is nice!

See, the problem is that God gives men a brain and a penis, and only enough blood to run one at a time.

Robin Williams

Salt & pepper, sugar & spice

chapter 6
Salt & pepper, sugar & spice

A Compatibility Questionnaire

I first came up with the idea for this exercise a couple of years ago when a television programme wanted me to counsel two celebrities who were about to get married. The programme wanted to see if there was a foolproof way to determine whether or not two people were perfectly matched. Well of course there isn't a guaranteed, impossible-to-fail way. If there were then there would be no divorce or separation and a lot less unhappiness around.

However what we can do is identify some possible areas that could cause us trouble down the road, and do a little 'preventative maintenance'. So think of this as surveying a piece of property that you are about to move into. You're probably going to buy it no matter what — you just need to know the how/what/where of repairs.

Please answer the questions separately on individual pieces of paper. And under no circumstance peek at the answers! When you're both finished then go through them together.

Enjoy!

The
Questions:

Section 1
DAY-TO-DAY

This section covers the nuts and bolts of your daily existence. Who likes to sleep with the window open, who never tidies up, who leaves the top off the toothpaste and the towels on the floor? Seemingly innocuous when you're deep in the throes of new love but often the first area where the cracks will start to show.

1 How do you find living with .... ?

2 What is his/her most annoying personal habit?

3 Have you told him/her about it and what did he/she say/do?

4 What is the best thing about living with .... ?

Section 2
MAKING THE COMMITMENT

This is about what made you decide to take the next step. Did you want to have a nice party; did someone need immigration papers, were the mammies looking for grandchildren? Important to be clear from the beginning as to 'why now' so that down the road you're not faced with 'well I never really wanted to do it and you made me'.

5   What made you finally decide to take the relationship to another level? You'd been perfectly happy where you were – what made you decide to do this? Did you feel pressurised in any way?

6   What would have happened if both of you were not in agreement about moving forward; would that have caused the end of the relationship?

Section 3
WHO IS THIS PERSON?

This is about your perception of this person in relationship to the outside world and your perception of them in relationship to you. 'Everyone thinks he's a thug because he's always punching people in the pub but I see a totally different side to him...'

7   What do you think are the best and worst qualities about .... in relationship to the rest of the world?
   ['She is always there for her family' but 'She never lets anyone get a word in edgeways'.]

8   What do you think are the best and worst qualities about .... in relationship to you?
   ['He is always there for me' but 'He shouts when he gets angry'.]

Section 4

THE MORAL MAZE

Relationships quite often fall down because people have very different moral values. This can become an enormous issue especially when children enter the equation.

9 Your partner is walking down the street and sees an envelope full of money on the footpath, what would he/she do with it? Take it to the police/buy himself that .... he's been after/spend it on gifts for you/other choice.

10 You're walking down the street and you see a group of kids harassing a pensioner what would you do? What would your partner do?

11 There's an election coming up shortly how important would that be to you? How important is that to .... ?

Section 5

TO TALK OR NOT TO TALK

This is the biggie. Communication. How you regard
communication and problem-solving; and how do you do it?

12 What are some of the things you argue about on
   a regular basis?

13 How do you argue? Sulking/shouting etc.

14 Who usually says sorry first?

15 How do you make up?

16 When the argument is over does ----------------------------
   move on or does he/she tend to hold on it and bring
   it up again and again?

17 Who starts the most rows?

18 Who usually backs down first?

Section 6
THE HARD TIMES

What do you do when the proverbial hits the fan? Do you work through it or do you ditch and move on?

19 What has been the biggest obstacle your relationship has had to overcome? How did you handle it?

20 Was there ever a time when you thought – right, this is it, and it's over?

21 What made you come back?

22 What is the one thing that .... could do that would make you walk away?

Section 7

HOW DEEP IS YOUR LOVE?

What makes you willing to do the work that needs to be done?

23 If your relationship were to end tomorrow what would you miss the most about .... ?

24 Close your eyes and try to imagine the rest of your life without .... in it — how does that make you feel?

The
Answers:

Please remember that there is no such thing as a right answer or a wrong answer. These are just guidelines to open up a conversation between the two of you so you can see if you can identify areas that might need a bit of work before they turn into fully-fledged problems.

You will notice that a few questions don't have accompanying answers. That is because those particular questions are just there to provide more background for that particular topic.

GOOD LUCK!

Section 1
DAY-TO-DAY

This section covers the nuts and bolts of your daily existence. Who likes to sleep with the window open, who never tidies up, who leaves the top off the toothpaste and the towels on the floor? Seemingly innocuous when you're deep in the throes of new love but often the first area where the cracks will start to show.

1 **How do you find living with .... ?**
   Often we take for granted how much we enjoy being with our partner. Reminding ourselves, and them, every now and then adds a bit of sparkle to the relationship.

2 **What is his/her most annoying personal habit?**
   Quite often, especially in the beginning of a relationship, people are cautious about expressing a dislike of anything at all about their new lover. That is understandable, however so is the complete surprise often shown by someone who had absolutely no idea that nothing puts you over the edge more than them going to sleep every night with the television blaring. And if he hasn't told you that the sound of you filing your fingernails makes him want to hide under the bed then you can end up in an enormous row, which could have been easily avoided by a simple conversation.

   In tackling this, it is important that you make the statement as mild and gentle as possible. 'I know you are used to being on your own and the television helps you fall asleep, however it has the totally opposite effect on me; do you think there is a compromise we can come up with?' As in any kind of situation it is helpful to come to the table with a possible solution. 'I have been checking out cordless headphones as a possibility, how would you like an early Christmas present?' A lot of this stuff sounds totally unimportant but you wouldn't believe how many times couples end up in front of me and when we start trying to get to the source of what ails their relationship it stems from a collection of what I call 'simple annoyances'.

3   **Have you told him/her about it and what did he/she say/do?**
How people handle these simple conversations will sometimes tell you a lot about possible future 'issues' in your relationship. Someone says 'I'm so, so sorry I had no idea. Yes, let's see what we can do about it'. Or 'You know you're right; I don't like listening to anyone else filing their nails either. No probs, I'll do it in another room or when you're not home'. Then you're on to a winner. However sulking, 'You're always nagging away at me', or focusing on the telly while you're talking might indicate you need to consider your position.

If you can't discuss simple things without it becoming a big issue then chances are you might find dealing with the big stuff just not workable or not worth it. This is a dangerous place to be because you then fall into the 'it's just not worth the hassle' syndrome. Not good. There is a thin line between calming down and letting everything roll off your back for the sake of peace and quiet – and letting every single thing in the world annoy you if it isn't done in the way you would like it to be done.

4 **What is the best thing about living with** .... ?
What you are looking for here is how quickly an answer springs to mind, and what type of answer it is. Is it 'Oh everything is wonderful but I guess waking up to her smiling face is the best'; or is it 'errrrrm let me think... (10 minutes later) ...well I guess, hmmm I don't know really'. This sort of answer is not a wrong/right answer (none of these are). It just means that you might need to spend a bit more time appreciating and being grateful for your other half's presence in your life.

Section 2
MAKING THE COMMITMENT

This is about what made you decide to take the next step. Did you want to have a nice party; did someone need immigration papers, were the mammies looking for grandchildren? Important to be clear from the beginning as to 'why now' so that down the road you're not faced with 'well I never really wanted to do it and you made me'.

5 **What made you finally decide to take the relationship to another level? You'd been perfectly happy where you were – what made you decide to do this? Did you feel pressurised in any way?**

It is really important to think this through and be clear about this if possible. Right now it might not seem important but later in the relationship at the first sign of trouble you don't want to hear 'Well I never wanted to do it anyway and you made me'. And while one of you might be more keen than the other – that's fine. One of you manipulating the other into moving in or getting married is very much not fine!

6 What would have happened if both of you were not in agreement about moving forward; would that have caused the end of the relationship?

Very tricky because you never want to look as if you are holding someone to ransom to get your own way. However it is also important that you are honest about what you need to happen to feel comfortable. There are too many relationships where one party really doesn't want to commit but goes along with new arrangements just to keep the peace. Or the other common situation where one person feels the need for a commitment but stays in the relationship against their will even though the other person won't commit. Either situation will end you up in a precarious position over time.

Section 3

WHO IS THIS PERSON ANYWAY?

This is about your perception of this person in relationship to the outside world and your perception of them in relationship to you. 'Everyone thinks he's a thug because he's always punching people in the pub but I see a totally different side to him...'

7 What do you think are the best and worst qualities about .... in relationship to the rest of the world? Name three of each: e.g. 'She is always there for her family' but 'She never lets anyone get a word in edgeways'.

Much of the time our partner shows the outside world a very different person from the one they show us. If you are someone who puts a lot of value in what other people think, this question might be hugely important to you.

8 What do you think are the best and worst qualities about .... in relationship to you? Name three of each: e.g. 'He is always there for me' but 'He shouts when he gets angry'.

It is really important that you have a solid perception as to the character of the person you are with. You need to know who they really are. It might not seem particularly important now when everything is ok but if the relationship hits a rocky patch it will be very helpful in aiding you to understand behaviour, which to you might be inexcusable or unexplainable.

Section 4
THE MORAL MAZE

Relationships quite often fall down because people have very different moral values. This can become an enormous issue especially when children enter the equation.

9 Your partner is walking down the street and sees an envelope full of money on the footpath, what would he/she do with it? Take it to the police/buy himself that .... he's been after/spend it on gifts for you/other choice.

A recent survey on morals found that our attitude towards what is acceptable and what isn't has changed radically over the years. For some this isn't an issue, for others it is.

10 You're walking down the street and you see a group of kids harassing a pensioner what would you do? What would your partner do?

How you regard your role in society might of great importance to you and if it is then the answer you get to this might carry a serious amount of weight.

11 There's an election coming up shortly how important would that be to you? How important is that to .... ?

Politics and social responsibility can also be a talking point. For example it would be very difficult for me to be with someone who had little or no interest in such matters, while it might not matter to you at all.

Section 5
TO TALK OR NOT TO TALK

This is the biggie. Communication. How you regard communication and problem-solving; and how do you do it?

12 **What are some of the things you argue about on a regular basis?**
This will help you see if there are certain areas of your relationship that need to be sorted out once and for all.

13 **How do you argue? Sulking/shouting etc.**
The way in which you argue is crucial in a serious relationship and has a lot to do with whether or not the relationship will have a longevity. (*See section on arguing effectively.)

14 **Who usually says sorry first?**
While it is important to apologise when it's necessary it is even more important that a) you really are sorry and not just paying lip service, and b) that you don't develop a pattern where one person always says sorry just to keep the peace.

15 **How do you make up?**
Not always s-e-x. Not always expensive gifts. Neither will work over the long run. Important to have a situation where simple and honest dialogue is more than enough to clear up a bad situation.

16 When the argument is over does ------------------------------
move on or does he/she tend to hold on it and bring
it up again and again?
If after an argument is over then one or the other of
you repeatedly brings it up again then it probably was
not properly cleared up. Go back and sit down at the
table again.

17 Who starts the most rows?
Is one of you always looking for a scrap? Maybe it's
possible that your communication techniques need some
work if you are having more 'scraps' than conversations.

18 Who usually backs down first?
Sometimes it is wise to concede the point but be sure that
however the situation has been resolved you both feel
that you have expressed yourself equally and been heard.

Section 6
THE HARD TIMES

What do you do when the proverbial hits the fan? Do you work through it or do you ditch and move on?

19 **What has been the biggest obstacle your relationship has had to overcome? How did you handle it?**
This is helpful to keep in the back of your mind so that when you come up against other obstacles you can either use methods that have proven successful in the past. Or avoid methods that didn't.

20 **Was there ever a time when you thought – right, this is it, and it's over?**
I don't want you to dwell on this. It just helps sometimes when things feel difficult to say to yourself 'Well we got over .... so this is a piece of cake'. In any serious relationship there are going to be tough times. The longer the relationship the more you will encounter. Learning to work through them together is one of the most useful tools any couple will ever have.

21 What made you come back?

It is really important that you have a solid perception as to the character of the person you are with and what your relationship is really all about. It might not seem particularly important now when everything is ok but if the relationship hits a rocky patch it is always helpful to be able to remind yourself what it is that you want to hold on to.

22 What is the one thing that .... could do that would make you walk away?

If there is something that you feel would be a dealbreaker it is important to let it be known in the beginning of the relationship. Not in a confrontational 'If you ever do this I will kill you!' kind of way. But in a quiet 'I think I need to explain that I have very strong feelings about x-y-z and if it happened it could have serious consequences to our relationship. Is there anything you feel that strongly about as well?

Section 7

HOW DEEP IS YOUR LOVE?

What makes you willing to do the work that needs to be done?

23 **If your relationship were to end tomorrow what would you miss the most about** .... **?**
This is more of appreciating and being grateful for what we have, something most of us just don't do enough of.

24 **Close your eyes and try to imagine the rest of your life without** .... **in it – how does that make you feel?**
Don't do this too often, as the feeling can be quite overwhelming. Sometimes when I do it I just burst out bawling. But even if you're not over-the-top emotional like me, thinking about life without your loved one will usually give you the energy that you need to keep moving forward.

Piglet sidled up to
Pooh from behind.
"Pooh!" he whispered.
"Yes, Piglet?"
"Nothing," said Piglet,
taking Pooh's paw.
"I just wanted to
be sure of you."

A.A. Milne

Dear Couples

Hopefully you will find that this simple
exercise has been as helpful to you as it has
to the many people I've worked through
it with. Take it as a template to make your
relationship stronger and remember, no one
else can tell you whether you're right for
each other or not – only your hearts can tell.

All the best

Jenni x

Index

'The Greatest Tips in the World' books

Baby & Toddler Tips
ISBN 978-1-905151-70-7

Barbeque Tips
ISBN 978-1-905151-68-4

Breastfeeding Tips
ISBN 978-1-905151-34-9

Cat Tips
ISBN 978-1-905151-66-0

Collecting Tips
ISBN 978-1-905151-42-4

Cookery Tips
ISBN 978-1-905151-64-6

Cricketing Tips
ISBN 978-1-905151-18-9

DIY Tips
ISBN 978-1-905151-62-2

Dog Tips
ISBN 978-1-905151-67-7

Etiquette & Dining Tips
ISBN 978-1-905151-21-9

Fishing Tips
ISBN 978-1-905151-33-2

Freelance Writing Tips
ISBN 978-1-905151-17-2

Gardening Tips
ISBN 978-1-905151-60-8

Genealogy Tips
ISBN 978-1-905151-72-1

Golfing Tips
ISBN 978-1-905151-63-9

Horse & Pony Tips
ISBN 978-1-905151-19-6

Household Tips
ISBN 978-1-905151-61-5

Personal Success Tips
ISBN 978-1-905151-71-4

Podcasting Tips
ISBN 978-1-905151-75-2

Property Developing Tips
ISBN 978-1-905151-69-1

Relationship & Dating Tips
ISBN 978-1-905151-35-6

Retirement Tips
ISBN 978-1-905151-28-8

Sex Tips
ISBN 978-1-905151-74-5

Slimming & Healthy Living Tips
ISBN 978-1-905151-31-8

Travel Tips
ISBN 978-1-905151-73-8

Wedding Tips
ISBN 978-1-905151-27-1

Pet Recipe books

The Greatest Feline Feasts in the World by Joe Inglis
ISBN 978-1-905151-50-9

The Greatest Doggie Dinners in the World by Joe Inglis
ISBN 978-1-905151-51-6

'The Greatest in the World' DVDs

The Greatest in the World – Gardening Tips
presented by Steve Brookes

The Greatest in the World – Yoga Tips
presented by David Gellineau and David Robson

The Greatest in the World – Cat & Kitten Tips
presented by Joe Inglis

The Greatest in the World – Dog & Puppy Tips
presented by Joe Inglis

For more information about currently available
and forthcoming book and DVD titles please visit:

www.thegreatestintheworld.com

or write to:

The Greatest in the World Ltd
PO Box 3182
Stratford-upon-Avon
Warwickshire CV37 7XW
United Kingdom
Tel / Fax: +44(0)1789 299616
Email: info@thegreatestintheworld.com

The author

Jenni Trent Hughes realised quite a few years ago that her life's calling was to help people enjoy a better quality of life. She has enjoyed careers as varied as geophysical technician for an oil company, corporate executive, painter, and writer but now she focuses on showing people how to be happy. She has been, and continues to be, agony aunt for several magazines and Internet sites. She has already published a book on difficult conversations and contributes regularly to magazines and newspapers. Jenni will be familiar to many of you from her extensive work in television from series like *Perfect Match* and *Loose Women* to *Toddler-Taming* and *This Morning*. She is a regular on *Grumpy Old Women* though she is neither grumpy nor old as you will surely by now have realised.

Jenni also produces programmes for BBC Radio 4 on subjects as diverse as men's relationships with their fathers to how people regard their passages through the decades of life. Her passions are travel, reading and music though she is considering giving it all up to move to Egypt and become a quad biking instructor. She lives in London with her son Jack and hopes that someday he will make someone a lovely husband.

Catlives

Catlives

Sarah Kirsch's KATZENLEBEN

Translated and edited

by Marina Roscher and Charles Fishman

Texas Tech University Press
1991

Originally published as *Sarah Kirsch Katzenleben: Gedichte*,
Copyright 1984 Deutsche Verlags-Anstalt GmbH, Stuttgart

This book was set in 10 on 13 Galliard and printed on acid-
free paper that meets the guidelines for permanence and
durability of the Committee on Production Guidelines for
Book Longevity of the Council on Library Resources.

Copyright 1990 Marina Roscher and Charles Fishman

Design by Joanna Hill
Jacket art *Waterscape* by Maureen Mahoney-Barraclough

Printed in the United States of America

Library of Congress Cataloging-in-Publication Data

Kirsch, Sarah.
    [Katzenleben. English & German]
    Catlives : Sarah Kirsch's Katzenleben / translated and edited by
Marina Roscher and Charles Fishman.
        p.   cm.
    English and German.
    Includes indexes.
    ISBN 0-89672-232-5 (c).—ISBN 0-89672-231-7 (p)
    I. Roscher, Marina.   II. Fishman, Charles M., 1942–
III. Title.
    PT2671.I758K3813   1991
833′.914—dc20   90-43324
                                                     CIP

Foreword

Catlives is an offering of Sarah Kirsch's poetry in English, rendered with a fidelity to her inventiveness in German that is perhaps only possible in collaborations such as this: between poet and scholar, poet and linguist. This is the work of translators who have deeply assimilated the labor of an intensely lyrical imagination. Kirsch begins with what is at hand, the sky coloring, snow in a field, and she follows the tenuous associative thread of her sensory intelligence, finding her concerns in things, rather than appropriating them to serve conscious intentions. Her work is whimsical and dramatic, but never degenerates into the idyllic meanderings of self-absorption.

An historical awareness acts as a magnetic field upon her thought. In "Stoneheart," the birds cry *human names over the field*. In "Oaks and Roses," a representation of her poetic consciousness, she moves from the purchase of a train station's timetable, through a landscape grounded in the American West, finally fusing Siberia with an elegiac vision of refugees or exiles. These, it seems to me, constitute evidence of the past, the Germany of her childhood, resonant within her, present within her, an inescapable mark of the darkness over which she maintains a vigil. Her poem "Snow" gives voice to her deep awareness of the precariousness of life, the world as it seems to us: *How before our practiced eyes / Everything changes the village flies / Centuries back in the snow / All we need are a couple of crows.*

That her poetry located itself in the natural world was a source of difficulty in her native East Germany, where she was accused of embodying in the language a certain passivity and resignation which was anathema to the articulated goals of the state. Her work was nontopical and overtly uncommitted. The criticism took another turn when she found herself under official attack for supporting the dissident poet Wolf Biermann (resulting in her exile to West Germany in 1977). The controversy surrounding her work seems now to have less to do with her poetic sensibility. It is rather a manifestation of the constraints of literary and political dogma.

Catlives aptly suggests her perception of the possibilities for survival. In one poem, kittens *Regularly before they reach the ladder rungs* fall headlong onto the flagstones of the cowshed, at which point *the gray siblings / Take over the explorer's teat / On the maternal belly their chances / To survive up more than a notch.*

Sarah Kirsch's cats appear throughout this collection: pregnant cats, sleeping cats, and she writes that *the poets love cats / The uncontrollable gentle / Free who laze away November rain / On silken seats or in rags / Sleeping dreaming and mute / Give their answer shake themselves and / Live on behind the huntsmen's fence / While zealous neighbors / Keep their eyes on license plates / The watched one inside his four walls / Long ago left the borders behind.* This is what it is, for Kirsch, to be a poet in a totalitarian state, and here she attests to the powers of imagination where behind the huntsmen's fence and under the eyes of the watchers, one can live—spiritually—without detection.

In this cycle of poems, the year in its seasons, we hear the voice of exile and poetic survival, celebration and cunning. It is perhaps fitting that they should be published as the Germany of her past and that of her present converge. It is perhaps a sign of hope that such poets as Sarah Kirsch have kept a light of poetic wisdom burning.

Carolyn Forché

Contents

Acknowledgments

Our thanks to the editors of the following journals, in which some of these translations, some in earlier versions, first appeared:

Cedarmere Review: "The Housing," "Inn"
Esprit: "Daybreak," "Frost"
The Hollins Critic: "Gentle Fright"
New Letters: "Blue Garden Ball," "Motionless,"
    "Stoneheart," "Winter Promenade"
Poetry Canada Review: "Last Day," "Movement"
Prism International: "Fish and Chips"
Rohwedder: "Fiery Oven," "The Geese Flew Inland," "The
    Geologists," "The Green Double," "Hoarfrost Harvest,"
    "Moorland," "When the Ice Floats"
Visions: "Breather," "Rainy Season"
Webster Review: "Damnation," "Gentle Hunt,"
    "Heartstone," "Ravens," "The Sleeper," "The Trochel"

Sarah Kirsch: An Introduction

Recognition of this poet is overdue in the United States and other English-speaking countries. Indeed, Sarah Kirsch, author of—at last count—nineteen books, is one of the finest contemporary European poets. Her many prizes and awards include the Petrarca Preis, the Friedrich Hölderlin Preis, the Stipendium of Villa Massimo, Rome, and the Staatspreis for European Literature, Austria.

Sarah Kirsch was born in 1935, in what is now East Germany. She studied biology and literature in Halle and Leipzig, and worked in a sugar factory. In 1977, political pressures forced her to move from East to West. The poet now lives in northern Germany, not far from the Danish border, where she and her loved ones share house and grounds with cats, dogs, a turtle, a donkey, and nine sheep. She continues to publish poetry and prose texts, as well as translations.

Kirsch's own linguistically innovative poetry is not easy to translate. It is intense. It has extraordinary richness and density. It bends language into new patterns. Punctuation is largely replaced by a breathpause in the line. This pause produces a rhythm which helps clarify the layered and substantive content. Subtle distortions of grammar and syntax serve to enlarge a poem's meaning. This special and highly controlled idiom may pose difficulties in the translations as it does in the deceptively simple German originals but, when read carefully, the intended obstacles to premature understanding, together with the colorful imagery, the associational thought, and the strong expressive movement, combine into a powerful poetic presence.

It is the imagery in particular that conveys the message in Kirsch's strikingly visual work. "There are few metaphors in my poems. Mostly, it's pictures," she herself says in an interview. Pictures, yes. Scenes that become events, settings on which she projects deep inner happenings— such are the 86 poems that constitute the sustained vision, the continuity, of Sarah Kirsch's *Catlives*.

In the present book, the course of four seasons experienced in a spare countryside provides the poet with opportunities for minute and intimate observations. She focuses on cats, cows, and dogs, on plants and leaves; she assigns to each grass and each weed its own place and its name. Overtly, the poems deal with nature, their environment is bucolic but, the reader soon understands, they are very far from idyllic. Here, "much goes on under ground," the fearful unknown arises from "black stripped gardens," and "the petrified forest shelters deathbirds." The uncanny dwells beneath the surface, and existence is threatened. Horror and anger, moments of resignation giving way to defiance, and love of nature, a nature Kirsch sees as already lost to us, inspire these poems. They have magic, a quality of fairytale that, as Günter Kunert points out, is used to convey the dreadful softly. Often, says Kunert, under cover of cheerful or tender language, they deliver a sting that is not immediately felt. The connotations of a single word, the surprising juxtaposition of a substantive and adjective, may suddenly chill, may expose dread hidden by a poem's naive-seeming surface.

Kirsch does not mince words. She gives us life as it is today, suffused with destructive and evil forces. But always her poems find the courage to face this life. Always, they reach for some formula of healing—perhaps, an incantation. In our world, where "man a mother's son / Stepped upon beaten a bastard goes past / Dark-red overflowing streams," cats and people do survive. They "live on behind the huntsmen's fence" because, in spite of everything, so we are promised, "after fire and ice the daffodils will / Bloom in the spring."

The poems in *Catlives,* then, reflect a constantly renewed commitment to life; they reflect the glory that is mankind's *courage to be*.

—Marina Roscher

Verschiedene Zeit

Am Morgen weidet der Nebel
Auf verlassenen Wiesen
Die Stimme des Zwerghahns
Steckt zwischen Tür und Angel.

Die schönen Dächer geduckten Häuser
Näherten sich in der Kälte
Unbekanntes taucht auf aus
Schwarzen entblätterten Gärten

Im blassen Himmelsgewölbe
Des Vogelzugs alte Schrift
Aufwächst Tellerlands Mietengebirge
Plastiklaken buhlen um Schnee.

Different Time

In the morning haze grazes
On abandoned pastures
The voice of the woodcock is
Stuck between door and hinge.

The beautiful roofs cowering houses
Have drawn close in the cold
The unknown arises from
Black stripped gardens.

In the pale skies
Migration's old script
Up rears the tableland's tenement range
Plastic sheets wooing for snow.

Eichen und Rosen

Ich habe mir in Ferlinghettis Laden
Einen Fahrplan gekauft und sitze im Pullman-Waggon
Und fahre die Küste ab Tag und Nacht und der Dichter
Spiegelt seinen Kuhschädel im Fenster wir fahren
Auf ewig nach Wyoming rein Zeile für Zeile Mann
O Mann ist das ein Tempo und ich sehe ihn mit einer
Krimmerfellmütze in einem Blechdorf die schwankenden
Telegrafenmaste kippen gleich um und die Straßen-
Kreuzer heulen wie Wölfe, auf einer Kreuzung.
Die Welt ist ein Gehöft im Winter wir kommen
Nicht rein fliegender Nebel wenn ich zum Fenster gehe
Und die herrlichen Bäume in Deutschland
Wandern als amerikanische Eichen glühend vorbei
Auf den presbyterianischen Kirchhöfen modern Rosen
Und sein Gedicht knallt weiter Schienenstöße
Böse böse reden schwerverständliche Krähen
Und als es extrem dunkel geworden ist und wir uns
Unübersehbar wohl und Steppe im Blick weiße Heide
In der Transkyrillischen Bahn befinden, komm
Ins Offene Freund und Leben rückwärts buchstabieren
Fragen wir uns was aus den wilden Jungs Jewgeni Andrei
Inzwischen alles geworden sein kann und wir fliegen
Durch die unendlichen nichtabhörbaren Birkenwälder des
    Zaren
Lew Kopelew winkt uns ein Streckenarbeiter
Mitm Beutel schwarzer Heimaterde zu sein riesiger Kopf
Sein weißer Bart begleiten uns lange sind einfach nicht
Von der Scheibe zu wischen bevor der schöne Waggon
Auffährt in herbstlichen flammenden Flammen.

Oaks and Roses

I've bought myself a timetable in Ferlinghetti's
Store and I sit in the Pullman car
And ride along the coast day and night and the poet
Mirrors his cowhead in the window we ride
Endlessly into Wyoming line by line man
Oh man what a pace and I see him with an
Astrakhan cap in a tinplate village the tottering
Telegraph poles are just about toppling and the highway
Cruisers howl like wolves, on a crossing.
The world is a farmstead in winter we can't
Get in fog flies when I go to the window
And the magnificent trees in Germany
Hike by fiery as American oaks
Roses rot in Presbyterian graveyards
And his poem keeps cracking track-jolts
Wicked wicked talk abstruse rooks
And when it has gotten extremely dark and we find
    ourselves
Unbounded steppe in our view white heather
On the Transcyrillian Railway, come
Into the open friend and we spell live backwards
Ask what can have become of the wild boys Yevgeny
    Andrei
In the meantime and we fly
Through the boundless untappable birchwoods of the Czar
Lev Kopelev waves to us a track-layer
With a bag of black earth from home his giant head
White beard accompany us long can't be
Wiped off the pane before the beautiful wagon
Drives up in autumnal fiery flames.

Sanfter Schrecken

Der Himmel erinnerte mich
An weiße Veilchen die in der Mitte
Des Kelchs eine Spur Rosa zeigen
Sehr viele weiße Veilchen und ein paar blaue
Wieder war alles gründlich verwandelt
Geschliffene Klarheit vielfache Linien
Die Häuser sehr nah und ihr Innres
Lag durchsichtig vor mir ich sah
Bis in die Seele des Bäckers, die letzen
Erschrockenen Mücken wärmten die Füße
An meinem Fenster, jeder Halm
War geschärft frisch angespitzt und ich zählte
Nebenäste vierundzwanzigster Ordnung
Die Welt bestand aus Einzelheiten
Es war genau zu unterscheiden
Welches übriggebliebene Blatt
Um ein weniges vor oder hinter
Anderem leis sich bewegte.

Gentle Fright

The sky reminded me
Of white violets showing
A trace of pink in their cup
Very many white violets and a few blue
Again everything was profoundly changed
A cut clarity multiple lines
The houses close by their innerness
Laid clear before me I saw
Straight into the baker's soul, the last
Frightened gnats warmed their feet
On my window, every stalk
Was sharpened to a point and I counted
Offshoots to the twenty-fourth order
The world consisted of single parts
It was easy to distinguish
Which leftover leaf
Moved quietly just a bit before or behind
Another.

Kälte

Gedämpftes Hundebellen laternentragende
Kinder am Martinstag wenn der Heilige
Durchs Dorf und über die Felder reitet.
Die gesprungene Schüssel des Himmels
Die Straße unbedeutender niederer Sterne
So lange unerwiderte Liebe angenommenen
Gottes töten das Herz im Gemäuer der Nacht.

Cold

Muffled dogbarks lanterns carried
By children on Martin's day when the saint
Rides through the village and across the fields.
The cracked bowl of heaven
The path of insignificant low stars
So long unrequited love of the assumed
God slay the heart in the stonewalls of night.

Schnee

Wie sich vor unseren geübten Augen
Alles verwandelt das Dorf fliegt
Um Jahrhunderte rückwärts im Schnee
Es bedarf dazu einiger Krähen
Kopfweiden am Weg altmodische Hunde
Liebe und Treue gelten du ziehst mich
Über Gräben trägst mein gestohlenes
Bündelchen Holz in den Abend
Lebendiger Rauch hüllt die Dächer.

Snow

How before our practised eyes
Everything changes the village flies
Centuries back in the snow
All we need are a couple of crows
Pollard willows along the way oldfashioned dogs
Love and faithfulness count you pull me
Over ditches carry my stolen little
Bundle of wood into the evening
Living smoke wraps up roofs.

Der Schläfer

Wenn nun der Frost kommt krachende Kälte und Winde
    vom Norden
Spürt der Schläfer schon die eilge Bewegung der Luft
Hört den Eissturm im Traum die Stimmen der Raben
Wenn sie nach Eßbarem gleich eh der Himmel sich rötet
Über die Koppeln hüpfen und sich die Bissen abjagen.
Wahrnimmt er mit dem dritten Auge hinter der Stirne
Ein verändertes Licht und weiß daß üppiger Schnee
Liebend das frierende Pflanzenwolk zugedeckt hat
Väterlich schützend die fetten Zwiebeln schöner Narzissen
Lilien Ranunkeln daß sie später wenns an der Zeit ist
Unsere Gartenbeete verzieren mit flämischen Farben.
Und bevor er sich wohlgefällig die Decke zur Nase zieht
Stürzt ihn ein böser Kobold noch einmal ins städtische
    Mietshaus
Wo er lau und ohne jegliche Nachricht von draußen
Eingegraben gelegen hat im dumpfen Gemäuer.
Nirgendein himmlischer Schein drang ihm da unter die
    Lider
Von Etagen umgeben die jedes frische Lüftchen verboten
Tappte er ohne Jahreszeiten gänzlich im Dunkeln
Lichtschächte warfen höchstens das Rufen verwilderter
    Tauben
Schaurig verstärkt von Mauer zu Mauer ihm in die
    Kammer
Statt gewaltiger Kranichzüge Ende des Sommers
Innezuwerden hörte er alte hustende Nachbarn
Ihre Wasserspülung bedienen nie gab es Stille
Ewiges Dröhnen und Brausen ließ die Ohren erstarren.
Aber nun hört er den Sturm durch den Eichenhain fliegen
Jetzt dringt ihm Schlittengeläut ins erleichterte Herz.

The Sleeper

When now the frost comes crackling cold and winds from
    the north
The sleeper can already feel the quick movement of air
Hears the ice storm in a dream the voices of ravens
How they hop after food in the paddock just before the
Sky turns red snatching each other's morsels.
He perceives an altered light through the third eye
In his forehead and knows that abundant snow
Has covered the freezing plantfolk with love
Paternally shielding the fat bulbs of daffodils
Lilies and tulips that they may later when it is time
Grace our gardens with Flemish colors.
And before he complacently pulls the blanket to his nose
An evil gremlin has plunged him once more into the urban
    tenement
Where he has lain lukewarm and lacking news from
    outside
Buried in the stale stone walls.
No heavenly gleam could enter there under his eyelids
Surrounded by tiers that suppressed every breath of fresh
    air
He groped without seasons in the dark
Lightshafts at best threw him cries of pigeons
Weird and boosted from wall to wall into the cubbyhole
Instead of remarking at summer's end the crane's mighty
    flight he
Heard old coughing neighbors flush their toilets there was
    no peace
Unending roaring and din numbed his ears.
But now he can hear the storm fly through oak trees
Now the ringing of sleighbells surges in his unburdened
    heart.

Anhaltender Niederschlag

Die schöne dünne Oblate die Wintersonne
Vergebung der Sünden Gottes für Hagel-
Schlag grobe Blitze getroffenes Vieh
Blickt nicht in gefrorene Pfützen die Weiden
Trauern am Zaun Grau abermals Grau
Die einzige Farbe des Himmels so hängt er
Nieder tief in die leeren Äste
Unbeweglicher Bäume denn auch der
Lustige Bruder der Wind hat sich entfernt
Liegt irgendwo auf der faulen Haut.

Meine Unterhaltung ist sehr abwechslungsreich
Lauter Pißgesang einschläferndes Murmeln
Die weiche laue Luft steigt zum Himmel
Was ich je an Freuden erlebte
Büße ich ab unterm Dach ich glaube
Das ewige Rauschen macht mich verrückt
Auch daraus wird nichts es regnet
Anhaltend langweilig nützlich
Wie eine Fabrik es ist vollkommen sinnlos
Nach Regenbogen und Wasserhosen
Ausschau halten einen Sperling erwarten.

Continuing Precipitation

The beautiful thin wafer the winter sun—
Forgiveness for sins of God after hail
Uncouth lightning struck livestock—
Is not looking in frozen puddles the willows
Mourn by the fence gray on more gray
The sky's only color hangs
Down deep in the bare branches
Of motionless trees for even the
Joker the wind has gone off
Takes it easy someplace idling.

My entertainment is very diversified
Loud piss music a soporific murmur
The soft mild air rises up to the sky
Under the roof I do penance
For what I ever knew of joy I guess
The endless rustling is driving me crazy
Nothing comes of that either it rains
Persistently boring useful
Like a factory it doesn't make sense
To keep watching for rainbows and
Waterspouts to wait for a sparrow.

Vorläufige Verwurzelung

Auf den Kälberwiesen steht Wasser
Grasbüschelinseln und hüpfende Vögel
Eiskanten am ausgewachsenen Schneehemd
Die Elstern spiegeln sich schon und die Katzen
Gehen sanft ihrer Wege und jede
Zu anderer eigener Zeit sie schütteln
Die vorderen Pfoten sind majestätisch
Wie ein Sack Scherben klingen die Stimmen
Weidender Perlhühner und immer in Panik
Umgestürzte Schüsseln mit Füßen
Schlagen sie sich selbst in die Flucht

Die Sonne müht sich vergeblich
Der klaren Spiegel der Pfützen halber
Durch die Wolken gelangen im weit
Fortgeschrittenen Jahr, erschöpft sich
In großangelegten barbarischen Untergängen
So sieht die Erde am Ende des Tages
Ungewiß wie ein fremder Planet aus
Mehr noch in der folgenden Nacht
Sternbilder auf mathematischen Achsen
Die vertrauten nicht auszumachen im toten
Weltall oder untergegangen

Wenn ich eins finde muß ich so frei sein
An Raum und Zeit nicht länger zu denken
Sonst flögen die Sterne hart auseinander
Cassiopeia zerkrachte und ich
Hier auf der Kugel ach wassen Stäubchen
Mit meinen ausgeworfenen Ankern
Kindern Katzen Geliebten einhundert
Tulpenzwiebeln im Erdreich Ranunkel-
Händchen daß ich nicht ausreißen kann
Und mich der Irrsinn nicht anfällt

Temporary Attachment

In the calf-meadow stands water
Islands of grass tufts and hopping birds
Ice hems the outgrown snowshirt
The magpies already see their reflection
And cats go softly on their way
Each at another singular time they shake
Their front paws are majestic
The voices of grazing guinea fowl
Sound like potsherds in bags always
In a panic overturned bowls on feet
They chase themselves off

The sun is struggling in vain
On behalf of the puddles' clear mirrors
To reach through the clouds of the far
Advanced year, wears itself out in
Largescale barbaric declines
And the earth at the end of the day
Looks uncertain like a strange planet
Even more in the following night
Constellations on mathematical axes
The familiar ones can't be made out in the dead
Universe or have gone down

If I find one I must be allowed
To stop thinking of space and time
Or the stars would fly hard apart
Cassiopeia shattered and I
Here on the ball oh what a mote
With my cast anchors
Children cats lovers onehundred
Tulip bulbs in the ground small hands
Of buttercups so I can't run away
And madness won't seize me

Angehäufter nützlicher Tand
Schafe Post ertrunkener Dichter
Sensen und Sicheln verjährtes Gras
Gummistiefel für schaurige Moore
Schlüssel für Nichts und Wiedernichts
An fernen Küsten habe ich Schwalben
Wahrlich ein Hausstand der leben läßt

Teelöffel der unbekannten Urgroßmutter
Die Verbotenes dachte während ihr Blick
Ranken folgte auf dem silbernen Ding
Hin in den Stall ging Schön
Hühnchen Schön Hähnchen der unverantwortliche
Kuckuck flog übers Dach

Heaped up useful trifles
Sheep letters from poets who drowned
Scythes and sickles inveterate grass
Rubber boots for gruesome moors
Keys to nothing and nowhere
I have swallows on distant shores
Truly household goods to live on

The unknown great-grandmother's teaspoon
Her illicit thoughts when her eyes followed
Tendrils on the silver thing
That way to the stable went pretty
Hen and pretty rooster the irresponsible
Cuckoo flew over the roof

Dritter Wurf

Die jungen Katzen stürzen regelmäßig
Eh sie die Leitersprossen erreichen
Vom Heuboden ab auf das Pflaster des Kuhstalls.
Nach dem ersten Todesfall wirft der Bauer
Stroh unter die Luke die grauen Geschwister
Übernehmen am mütterlichen Bauch
Die Zitze des Wegbereiters ihre Chancen
Zu überleben sind sprunghaft gestiegen.

Third Litter

Regularly before they reach the ladder rungs
The kittens fall headlong from
The hayloft down to the flagstones of the cowshed.
After the first fatal crash the farmer
Throws straw under the hatch the gray siblings
Take over the explorer's teat
On the maternal belly their chances
To survive up more than a notch.

Winterpromenade

Mistdämpfe dumpfe fromme Halluzinationen
Die breiten Stirnen die Hörner unter den Locken
Gereihte heilige Kühe auf ihren Podesten
Die Stammutter die Blesse ein Stern
Die Balken und Pfeiler die nackten Wände
Ornamente verlassener Schwalbennester
Strahlenkränze um elektrische Lampen
Heu und Stroh in den Krippen klirrende
Ketten sanfte Blicke gemästeter Ochsen
Das überwältigte ängstliche neugeborene Kalb
Die Stammutter die Gottesmutter das Blut
Scharf von den Steinen gespült weiße Ströme
In der Höhe pulsieren durch gläserne Rohre
Motorengeräusch Milchkesselglocken
Mönchsgesang Sturm wirft sich gegen die Türen

Winter Promenade

Dung fumes musty pious hallucinations
The broad forehead the horns under curls
Rows of holy cows on their pedestals
The matriarch the blaze a star
The beams and pillars naked walls
Ornaments of abandoned swallows' nests
Haloes around electric lamps
Hay and straw in the cribs clinking
Chains the fatted oxen's meek looks
The subdued frightened newborn calf
The matriarch God's mother the blood
Hosed sharply off the stones white streams
Above throbbing through glassy pipes
Motor noise milker bells
Monkish songs storm hurls itself at the doors.

Reglos

Der Tag kommt an aus den Wäldern
Unsichtbar es schneit in die Grenzen
Von gestern und heute ich kann
Auf der Erde nichts unterscheiden
Alles ist ununterscheidbar und gleich
Die Spuren der Wölfe der Lämmer
Die erfrorenen Hasen deckt Schnee
Er legt sich auf umgeblasene Bäume
Die lebenden will er ersticken
Er läßt die Bäche verschwinden
Moore und Teiche Felder alles ist
Gleich tot und begraben im Dämmerlicht
Sinkender drehender Schnee die Augen
Verwirren sich schwarze Flocken
Asche fällt nicht steigt auf oder der Himmel
Läßt sich herab weil die Geschöpfe sich ducken
Atemlos reglos die Stille wesenlos mondlos
Es ist nicht hell und wird nicht dunkel
Niemand geht auf den Feldern die Felder
Totenfelder wachsen hirtenlos stündlich
Der Schneefall dauert lang wie mein Leben
Ich habe den Namen der Ortschaft vergessen
Und die Straßen aufgehobenen Plätze
Wir befinden uns kurz nach dem Frieden
Wir können uns nicht erinnern was
Alles geschah das ausgelöschte Bewußtsein
Menschenleer gedankenlos kein Licht
Kein Schatten gepunktete Bilder und nur
Die Kraft sich nicht zu bewegen.

Motionless

The day comes out of the woods
Invisible it snows into the borders
Between yesterday and today I can't
Distinguish anything on earth
Everything is indistinct and the same
The tracks of wolves of lambs
The snow covers frozen hares
It lays itself on fallen trees
Wants to smother the living
Makes the brooks disappear
Moors and ponds fields everything
Dead and buried alike in the feeble light
Sinking spinning snow the eyes
Get confused black flakes
Ash does not fall but rises or the sky
Stoops down because the creatures cringe
Breathless motionless the silence incorporeal moonless
It is not light and does not get dark
No one walks in the fields the fields
Graveyards grow by the hour shepherdless
The snowfall continues as long as my life
I have forgotten the name of the place
And the streets the rescinded squares
We are shortly after the conclusion of peace
We cannot remember what
All happened the blotted consciousness
Deserted thoughtless no light
No shadow dotted pictures and only
The strength not to move.

Schonzeit

Maulfaul eine fremde Sprache sprechend die nur
Das Viehzeug versteht fuhrwerke ich mich
Hin durch den Winter mal weiß mal grün
Fällt er hier vor die Füße gestern reicht er
Mirn Hundsveilchen fast ein Schmetterling her
Heute hat er alles mit Schnee überworfen
Dreierlei Krähen wie sie im Buche stehn
Flattern Erbarmen heischend vorm Fenster
Ich schneide den abergläubischen Tieren
Rotbäckige Äpfel auf und erfahre
Den Ausgang der Treibjagd eine wahre
Friedensfeier und übermorgen ist Schonzeit
Die Bauern murren sich was in die Pelze kein Schwein
Diesen Winter nur ein paar Ratten und
Bilche die Hasen in ihren stolzen Gewölben
Weißesten Schnees erzählen von früheren Zeiten
Als *sie* die Jäger noch jagten was die für
Komische Haken schlugen ich geh
Übern Schnee ich geh über das fette
Österliche Gras Anfang des Jahres seh die
Bäche fürchterlich schwellen und leichte
Brücken aufheben später sind es
Häuser und Kinder und der Winter
Fängt erst an sagt der Häher oder der
Langbekannte Pferdekopf sommers wie
Winters hängt der aus dem Fenster und redet
Von härteren Zeiten in denen die flachen
Menschen ihrer wieder bedürfen
Große Zeiten mit Zaumzeugherstellern wenn der Komet
In dieses Sonnensystem hineinfliegt viel Feuer
Sagt er voraus und bläst mir Rotz auf die Backe
„Un na Füür un Ies bleiht int Fröhjahr de
Zittlöschen" dermaßen gestärkt und getröstet
Fällt es mir leicht ins Holzhaus gelangen
Die Türen schließe ich dicht und die Fenster
Eisblumen leuchten mich an auf den Dielen.

Closed Season

Buttoned up speaking a foreign language only
The animals understand I haul myself
Through the winter now white now green
It falls at the feet here yesterday
Hands me a violet almost a butterfly
Today has thrown snow over everything
Three kinds of crows straight out of a book
Flutter begging for alms at the window
I cut red-cheeked apples for the gullible
Animals and am told the results
Of the chase a genuine
Celebration of peace and tomorrow it's closed
Season the farmers are grumbling no luck
This winter a couple of rats and
Dormice the hares in their fine cellars
Under the whitest snow tell stories about
Bygone days when *they* still hunted the hunters
Funny the turns and doubles they'd take
Across the snow I walk over fat
Eastergrass at the beginning year see the
Brooks swell fearsome lifting
Light bridges later it's
Houses and children and winter has only
Begun says the jay or the
Familiar horse-head summers and
Winters that hangs in the window and speaks
About harder times when
People will need them again
Great times with bridlemakers when the comet
Flies into our solar system much fire he
Predicts and blows snot at my cheek
"And after fire and ice the daffodils will
Bloom in spring" thus strengthened and consoled
I find it easy to enter the wooden house
I shut up doors and windows and
Iceflowers gleam at me in the halls.

Das Gehäuse

Es ist dunkel im Haus Wassergardinen
Fließen vor den Fenstern bis zum Dreikönigstag
Wird die Weihnachtstanne geduldet
Auf den Lichtstümpfen zucken die Flammen
Wind drückt das dichtgefaltete Wasser
Eng an die Scheiben es blühen die
Zwiebelgewächse weiß blau und rosa
Die Dunkelheit fällt aus den Ecken
Schleicht über die Schwellen verkriecht sich
In sich selbst und unter die Betten
Die Stille quillt aus Truhen und Schränken
Und in der warmen greifbaren Düsternis
Die ich durchstoße die sich hinter mir schließt
Die wie violetter Samt herumhängt sich
Aufrollt und bläht in jedem Topf sitzt
Traktiert der den ich liebe plötzlich den Flügel
Mit zu Tränen rührenden Stücken
Die Katze kippelt auf ihrem Lieblingsstuhl
Die Dachrinnen laufen über an den
Vorbestimmten Stellen die betrunkene Seele
Des Zimmermanns klappert im Dachstuhl.

The Housing

It is dark in the house water curtains
Flow in front of the windows until Epiphany
We put up with the Christmas tree
Flames flicker on candle stubs
Wind presses the linenfold water
Close to the panes bulbous plants
Flower white blue and pink
Darkness tumbles from corners
Steals over sills creeps into
Itself and under the beds
Silence wells up from cupboards and coffers
And in the warm and tangible gloom
Through which I pass as it closes behind me
That hangs about like violet velvet
Rolls itself up and swells and sits in each pot
The one I love suddenly treats the piano
To pieces that move me to tears
The cat treads on her favorite chair
The drainpipes leak at the
Predetermined spots the carpenter's
Drunken soul is clattering in the rafters.

Der grüne Doppelgänger

Der Himmel bezog sich flatterndes Dunkel
Steht über dem Sumpfloch vollgetrunkenes
Torfmoos hängt sich erschreckend und schwer
An meines Wiedergängers Füße der sich
Nicht fürchtet unter den Fittichen dunkler
Kriechender Wolken und doch vergeblich
Nach dem Abendstern ausschaut nun schöpft er
Atem und sucht seine einzige Seele
In vielen Wasserspiegeln Kreise zu Kreisen
Geordnet schwarze Beeren abgestorbene Halme
Das rostrote Wasser leuchtet und dampft

Ich stelle die Lampe ins Fenster erwarte
Den Abtrünnigen Stunde um Stunde
Sehe ihn allerwege den treulosen
Unseßhaften flüchtigen Flüchtling
Verknotete Haare zerkratztes Gesicht
Nasse Fußspur verwilderte Worte
Schwenkt Teufelskralle und Rautenzweig
Spiegelt sich schon in der Scheibe geht
Durch das Glas mir in den Leib ist in
Wirklichkeit untergekommen.

The Green Double

The sky's become overcast a fluttering darkness
Stands over the marsh pool soggy
Peatmoss clings alarming and heavy
To my Doppelgaenger's feet who isn't
Afraid beneath the wings of the dark
Creeping clouds and yet looks in vain
For the evening star now he draws
Breath and searches for his singular soul
In the mirrors of many waters circles ordered
Into circles black berries dead stalks
The russet water glows gives off smoke

I put the lamp in the window await
The renegade hour by hour
See him everywhere the faithless
Unsettled runaway refugee
Hair tangled in knots face scratched up
Wet footprints wild words
Brandishing nightshade and branches of rue
He's already reflected in the pane comes
Through the glass into my body has found the real
Refuge.

Der Winter

Purpurfahnen. Roter Rauch aus den Häusern.
Verrückte ausgepreßte Seelen fahren auf.
In Sonnenblut getauchte Korallenwälder.
Rote Treppen am Himmel die Krähen
Fliegen von Stufe zu Stufe Herzkrähen
Vor Gottes uneingenommenen Thron.

Winter

Purple flags. Red smoke out of houses.
Crazy pressed souls rising up.
Coral woods bathed in sunblood.
Red stairs in the sky crows
Flying from step to step heartcrows
To God's unoccupied throne.

Machandelboom

Tagealter Nebel ich stecke im Sack
Rückwärts laufen die Uhren im Spiegel
Mausgraue Leute verspielen bei Licht
Flugs meine Hoffnung wolln mir darob
Schuld verschreiben der schöne Soldat
Eine Knochenpfeife zugeben.

Machandelboom

Daylong fog I'm stuck in the sack
Backwards run the clocks in the mirror
That sheds light on mousegray people
Quick to gamble away my hope wanting
To pass me indebtments for it the handsome
Soldier a bonefife thrown in.

The Machandelboom is the juniper of Grimms' Fairy Tales.

Waldstück

Der Nordwind zerstückelt die Wolken
Sie fahren über den Himmel bis in die
Wölfischen Tundren die Sonne steigt auf
Was sie an den Tag bringt verrammelte
Wälder abgebrochene Hütten im Dickicht
Die Tränen der Demonstranten kein Gras
Wächst darüber legt sich Beton.

Forest Piece

The northwind cuts up the clouds
They ride across the sky as far as the
Wolfish tundras the sun is rising
What he brings to light barred shuttered
Woods and battered huts the tears of
Demonstrators in the thicket no grass
Grows over it settles concrete.

Herzstein

Wenn die Häuser kein Strahl trifft
Nehmen sie die Farben
Umgebender Wolken Gewitterwände
Gnadenloser Feldsteine an
Ausgegangene Backöfen Trauer
Innen und Außen. Ein Ameisenhaufen
Wimmeln die Gedanken im Kreis
Um das Gerippe gestrigen Tags
Kein Stein fällt vom Herzen einem andern
Ins Brett blinde Flecken
Hindern den Blick durch die Scheiben.

Heartstone

When no sunbeam strikes the houses
They take on the colors of
Surrounding clouds stormfronts
Merciless fieldstones
Baking ovens gone cold grief
Inside and out. An anthill of
Thoughts teeming in circles
Around yesterday's skeleton
No pawn falls from the heart onto another's
Gameboard blind spots
Obstruct the view through the panes.

Moorland

Erst springe ich über die Gräben
Die seidenen Unterröcke leuchten
Im rostbraunen Wasser der Wind
Bläst mich von Sode zu Sode im Kreis
Roter niedergeschlagener Gräser
Blasen steigen auf aus den Tümpeln
Grünfunkelndes Moos es keuchen
Die zerbrochenen sinkenden Erlen
Speckige Pilze Koboldkanzeln
Bedecken flatternde Maste
Wie Patronen glänzt der Kot wilder Tiere
Der blitzgespaltene kopflose Stamm
Stellt sich mir in den Weg
Mit ausgebreiteten flehenden Armen
Die Ratte die ehdem mein Gutsherr war
Läuft voran auf befestigten Boden.

Moorland

First I leap across the trenches
In the rustbrown water silken
Petticoats shine the wind
Blows me from sod to sod in a circle of
Red downcast grasses
Gasbubbles rise from the ponds
The moss glitters green the broken
Sinking alders are panting
Greasy mushrooms the pulpits of goblins
Cover fluttering masts
The droppings of animals gleam like cartridges
Cleft by lightning the headless stem
Stands in my way
With outstretched beseeching arms
The rat who before was my lord of the manor
Runs and is first with his feet on firm ground.

Kunstwelt

Die eilfertige Wintersonne
Hat dem Korn Schaden getan
Frost zerstörte die Wurzeln
Die Felder leblose Teiche.
Ein Wolkenpetersdom spiegelt sich
Niederländische schwarze Krähen
Schlagen die Flügel.

Artworld

The rash winter sun
Has harmed the grain
Frost ravaged roots
The fields lifeless pools.
A cloud St. Peter's Dome looks
In the mirror Dutch black rooks are
Beating their wings.

Schneelose Zeit

Ende Januar in frostklaren Nächten
Setzen die langwierigen Saturnalien
Der ungebundenen Dorfkatzen ein Schreie
Daß dem Menschen die Knochen frieren.
Später bespringen sich Autos die Pfauen
Brülln fürchterlich diese Sucht
Die Welt mit Pfaueneiern belegen
Und Ochsen erwürgen sich
In dumpfer Erinnerung es ist die
Schneelose Zeit in der die Erde
Einen Aschemantel herzeigt die Gänse
Das Land aus den Lüften betrachten
Viel Unterirdisches sich zuträgt
Die Gasfackel über dem Moor steht.

Snowless Times

On frost-clear nights towards the end of
January begin the prolonged
Saturnalia of the licentious
Village cats screams
To make your bones freeze
Later on coupling cars the peacocks
Howling fearfully this craze to
Cover the world with peacock eggs
And oxen choke on their
Dulled memories it is the
Snowless time when the earth
Shows a mantle of ash geese
Look at the land from the air
Much goes on under ground
Over the swamp the gas-torch appears.

Kopfrechnen

Der weiße Nebel ist dem grauen gewichen
Die abgesonderten Höfe die leuchtenden
Mistplätze wenigen bunten Hähne
Vermögen nichts gegen die Trauer
Nach Wattenmeer riecht es zer-
Brochenen Deichen Wintertragödien
Verschollene Namen nach Jahren
Taucht der Mantelknopf auf Not
Schleust der Nebel in niedere Häuser
Die Kälber verscheißen sich und die Milch
Wird flockig graue Geschwüre
Liegen die Felder die räudigen
Wiesen randvoller Unglück schwarz
Rauchende Bäche ohne Bewegung.
Eine Mattigkeit sondergleichen
Ließ Flüche und Seufzer verstummen Stille
Dröhnt in den Ohren mit Maulwurfsgesichtern
Sitzen Greise hinter herabfallenden
Schweren Gardinen zählen die Gräber.

Mental Arithmetic

The white fog has yielded to gray
The secluded farms the gleaming
Dungheaps the few bright cocks
Can't alleviate the grief
It smells of shoals shattered
Dikes winter tragedies
Forgotten names the coat-button reappears
After many years fog sluices
Plight into the low houses
The calves have the shits and the milk
Turns flaky the fields lie ulcerous
The scabby meadows brimful
With bad luck black
Steaming brooks that don't move.
An unequalled lassitude
Silenced curses and sighs quietness
Roars in all ears the aged sit
Molefaced behind dropping
Heavy curtains counting graves.

Wenn das Eis geht

Das schöne Mühlrad in meinem Kopf
Unaufhaltsam dreht es sich eingedenk
Mit seinen Schaufeln Versunkenes heben
Es überschlägt sich der Strom hinter den Augen
Ist trübe und klar Strohpantoffeln
Abgeschnittene Locken Heiligenbilder
Treiben darin ersäufte Katzen und
Freundesleichen zuhauf viel Spreu wenig
Weizen gelangt auf den Mühlstein mitunter
Stöhnt das Getriebne bleibt stehn
Was sich verfangen hat bricht mir
Womöglich das Herz mein Mühlbach
Ist ohne Vernunft wenn das Eis geht
Das Rad dreht durch wirbelt Gelächter
Mir in den Leib lockere Sprossen
Schlagen das Unglück kaputt die Schwalben
Fliegen zum einen Ohr rein zum anderen
Raus

When the Ice Floats

The pretty mill wheel in my head
Goes round unflagging shovels
Mindful to raise what sank down
The stream behind my eyes turns over
Is murky or clear straw slippers
Cut off curls the pictures of saints
Drift in it drowned cats together with
Corpses of friends much chaff little
Wheat gets to the millstone sometimes
The workings groan and stop
What entangled itself may well
Break my heart when the ice floats
My millstream is without reason
The wheel spins empty laughter whirls
Into my body loose paddles
Knock bad luck to pieces the swallows
Fly into my ears and back
Out

Reif

Die Tage sind endlos weiß der Eismond
Die Schneesonnen ziehen im Nebel
Viel Rauhreif fliegt an legt sich
Um Zweige Gräser und Schilf
Jeden Spinnfaden hebt er leuchtend hervor
Schlittenleinen Fransen und Troddeln
Erschafft er an einem einzigen Morgen
Wächst den Bäumen strahlendes Laub
Stäubt wenn mittags die Schneekönigin
Von den Magnetgebirgen herabfährt
Ach sie will dich mir wegführn fürn
Paar Schlittschuh Eisvogelflügel
Ich schlage sie glatt in die Flucht
Mit Flintenschüssen da lenkt sie
Nach Jütland ein läßt noch
Den See zerspringen

Der weiße Wald reicht in den Himmel
Übergangslos verliern sich die Äste
Die schneeblinden Augen erholn sich
Bei frischen Maulwurfshügeln und Krähen
Der japanische Kirschblütengarten
Ein weißes endloses Schneewehpoem
Kälte und Schönheit ein verdecktes
Schlachtfeld ausgelöschte Schritte
Und wie Inseln darin verschiedene Haikus
Die Taube im Käfig des Reifbaums
Flattert ein klopfendes Herz
Der Eismond die Schneesonnen
Wühlen sich vor aus dem Milchwald
Aus den Zweigen stürzen Lawinen
In weißen Säcken herab auf deren Grund
Blei liegt.

Hoarfrost Harvest

The days are endless white the icemoon
The snowsuns drift in the fog
Much hoarfrost comes coating
Twigs grasses and reeds
Traces each spider's thread with sparkle
Makes ropes for sleds fringes and tassels
All in one morning
Grows gleaming leaves for the trees
Sprays powder at noon when the Snow Queen
Drives down from the magnetized mountains
Oh she's trying to take you away in exchange for
A pair of skates kingfisher's wings
But I chase her with musket shots
She cracks the lake and takes off
Toward Jutland

White forest fades into the sky
The branches blend without a break
The snowblind eyes rest on
Fresh molehills and crows
The Japanese garden of cherry blossoms
A white and endless snow-woe poem
Cold and beauty a concealed battlefield
Steps rubbed out
And like islands in it several haiku
The dove in the cage of the frost-tree
Flutters a beating heart
The icemoon the snowsuns
Burrow out from the milkwood
Avalanches crash from branches
In white sacks that are weighted
With lead.

Tempus hibernum

Wenn die Verzauberung nachläßt der Frost
Eine Pause macht Kräfte sammelt die Wiesen
Fast wie im Sommer liegen der Schnee
Ein dreckiger Rest ist auf glänzenden Teichen
Schmelzwasser steht wenn das Dorf
Seine Stalltüren öffnet die vorjährigen Kälber
Einen Nachmittag traben dürfen und es rundum
Nach Mist Kuhstall und Maismieten riecht
Wenn die Bauern im Wald Holz schlagen die Spechte
Im Garten versammelt sind die Sonne bedächtig
Und eingeschrumpft im immerwährenden Nebel
Hinfällig doch früher den Gang in den Äther wagt
Eine Dorfausgabe eine einfache nützliche
Sonne von der man noch hören wird
Wenn die Felder ihre Vornehmheit ablegen
Die Verwahrlosung sich herzeigt zusammengestürztes
Gewöhnliches Dasein Mistfladen vom vergangenen
    Sommer
An Ort und Stelle erscheinen Baumruinen
Unter tollwütigen Wolken vagabundieren
Die schwarzen Seelen der Krähen
Auffahren im Wind wenn das Leben
Also eintönig trist und vulgär ist
Unter unholden mürrischen Menschen bin ich
Froh in landläufiger Gegend.

Tempus hibernum

When the spell wanes and the frost
Takes a break to gather strength the meadows
Lie almost as if in summer the snow
Dirty dregs melts on the gleaming
Ponds when the village opens
The cowshed doors letting last year's calves
Run for one afternoon and it smells
All over of dung barns and cornstacks
When the farmers cut timber in the forest
The woodpeckers gather in the garden when the sun
Cautious and withered by constant fog
Feeble yet sooner dares the path into the ether
A village edition a simple useful
Sun from whom we'll hear more
When the fields lay aside their refinement
The raggedness showing itself crumpled
Everyday existence last summer's cow chips
Appear here and now wrecks of trees
Roam about under frenzied clouds
The black souls of crows
Rise up in the wind when life
Therefore is tediously sad and vulgar
Among unfriendly peevish people then I am
Glad of the countryside's ways.

Fish and Chips

Das holde Gestirn wenn es zu Tag tritt
Himmlische Agitation in Purpur und
Gold jagt schon Wärme ins Kreuz
Einen Mond später werd ich vor Gäa
Auf den Knien mich befinden bei
Grüner Farb Schnittlauch und Veilchen.

Fish and Chips

Already the gracious star when it dawns
Heavenly agitation in scarlet and
Gold is driving heat into the loins
One more moon and I'll be
On my knees before Gaea in
Green and violets and chives.

Lichtmeß

Mutmaßliche Kälte treibt die Sperlinge
Gottes windzerblasene Haferkörner
In Scharen durch die Zäune über die Wiesen.
Der scharfe Nordwind der Messerstecher
Trennt die Lebenden von den Toten.
Es zeigen sich allerorten die bärtigen
Fichten des Waldes und Trinker
Mit Kaninchenaugen streben dem Dorf zu.

Candlemas

Must be cold that sweeps the sparrows
God's windblown oat grains
In hordes through the fences across the fields
The sharp northwind the cutthroat
Divides the living from the dead.
The bearded firs of the forest
Show themselves everywhere and drunkards
With rabbit eyes make for the village.

Letzter Tag

Einer hat Einem
Geknicktes Stroh
Auf die Schwelle gelegt
Die klappernden Güllekessel am Morgen
Die Verzweiflung des Glöckchens
Wenn der Klauenschneider
Seinen Korn in die Milchkammer stellt.

Last Day

Somebody
Has put broken straw
On somebody's doorstep
The kettles of dung-water rattling
In the morning the despair of the little bell
When the hoof-cutter
Chills his rye in the milk house.

Gasthaus

Seit Tagen fällt der Regen so dicht
Und gleichzeitig steigt Nebel herauf
Daß die Welt wahrhaftig sehr klein
Und zusammengeschrumpft vorliegt
Sie reicht knappe drei Meter
Von der Traufe zum Misthaufen hin
Wird seitlich von fallenden
Zäunen und Himbeerruten begrenzt
An denen Tropfen wie Tränen
Fließen Pfützen verschmelzen
Bis das Meer vor der Tür steht.
Ein ordentliches Oben der hohe
Aufgestockte wolkenbefahrene Himmel
Ist nicht auszumachen es bleibt
Nur Fluchen und Türenwerfen
Oder die Kunst in sich selbst
Verloren zu gehen wie rings
Die frühen Hunde und Trinker.

Inn

For days now the rain has been falling so dense
While at the same time fog mounted up
That the world exists in fact
Very small and shrunken
It reaches barely ten feet
From the downspout to the dungheap
Is bound at the sides by toppling
Fences and raspberry canes
Weeping teardrops puddles
Merge until the sea stands at the door.
A regular Above the high
Storied cloud-travelled sky
Can't be made out nothing remains
But swearing and slamming of doors
Or the art to get lost
In oneself just like the early
Dogs and drunks.

Der Trochel

Verbogenes Holz das der Wind
Atemlos überfällt und verläßt
Nebel und Wolken ziehn
Durch die ausgebreiteten leeren
Häupter und Vögel und Blitze
Fahren hinein Seufzer
Hingegangenen abgestorbenen Lebens.

Alles war hier vor langer Zeit.
Der zugeschüttete Teich ist gewandert
Den verlassenen Hof hat der Wald
Geduldig zurückgenommen.
Das schwarze Huhn auf der Lichtung
Zeigt sich am Mittag und scharrt
Nach Ohrringen aus Dukatengold.

The Trochel

Twisted woods the wind
Out of breath assaults and quits
Mist and clouds pass
Through the open empty
Heads and birds and lightning
Flash in the sighs of
Passed and withered life.

Everything here was long ago.
The jammed pond has wandered
Forbearing the forest has taken
Back the vacant farm.
The black hen shows itself
In the clearing at noon scratching
For earrings of ducat gold.

The Trochel is a small local forest in northern Germany.

Falscher Hase

Die Felder sehen bereitwillig aus
Vögel in kahlen Alleen
Versuchen Sommergesänge trunkene Wagen
Torkeln über die Wiesen pissen sorgsam
Alte Grasbüschel ein süßer Geruch
Ohnegleichen hängt überm Dorf friedlich
Ruhigen Bauchs schläft der Vielfraß
Unter ehrwürdigen Steinen, die Schwalben
Fehlen an allen Ecken und Enden.
O ihr guten versunkenen leichtsinnigen
Seelen und Blumen bleibt in schützender
Trübsal wider die scheinheilige Sonne.

Canard

The fields look ready
Birds try out summer songs in
Bare trees tipsy carts
Reel over the pastures pissing with care
Old tufts of grass a sweet matchless
Scent hangs about the village the wolverine
Belly calm sleeps peaceful
Under ancient stones, the swallows are
Missing at every turn.
Oh you good sunken reckless
Flowers and souls stay sheltered in
Gloom against the spurious sun.

Die Heide

Die Sonne blendete mich ich ging
Auf irischer Heide
Schnepfenvögel eilige klappernde Flügel
Trugen Herzklopfen ein
Birken schlugen mir grob auf den Rücken
Von weitem hörte ich
Äxte stürzende Bäume
Eine Zeitung die ich nicht lesen konnte
Trieb im Wind, aus den Dünen
Kamen Gestalten mit lichten Haaren
Augen wie Sterne schwebenden Füßen
Wie sie in alten Büchern
Beschrieben werden schossen sich nieder.

The Moor

The sun blinded me I walked
Over Irish moors
Snipes quick chattering wings
Brought on palpitations
Birches slapped me hard on the back
From afar I heard
Hatchets crashing trees
A newspaper I couldn't read
Drifted in the wind, from the dunes
Came shapes with shining hair
Eyes like stars hovering feet
Such as are described in old
Books shot each other down.

Die Gänse flogen landeinwärts

Wenn der Winter sich wiederherstellt nachdem
Er zwei Wochen die Zügel schleifen ließ
Sonnige Lotterwirtschaft bei geöffneten Türen
Eine Fatamorgana endloser Wiesen die Bauern
Flogen darüber auf flügelstarken krähenden
Treckern allerhand Scheinverrichtungen
Vorzunehmen mit mehreren Hängern
Nun erheben sich an ihrer Stelle
Schwarze Vogeltürme der Sturm bläst sie auf
In niedere Wolken Schnee deckt
Die aschenfarbene Erde den Leichnam
Unter eingesunkener langverfaulender Haut.

Wenn wir zur Tür laufen nach Schritten
Ist es immer vergeblich nur der schneidende
Wind der anhaltende gleichmäßige
Feingemahlene Schnee liegen davor
Schwarze spöttische Augen die Finsternis.
Wir sind hier auf Jahre begraben
Sitzen am Schneefeuer und taun
Unsere schwarzgefrorenen Seelen auf.
Lilienfelder scheint uns das Weiße
Nun schon zu sein wir sind ganz benommen
Vom vielen Wacholder dem fetten Fleisch
Frischgeschlachteter Schweine im Rauch.

The Geese Flew Inland

When the winter gets a new grip on the reins after
Keeping them slack for two weeks
Sunny slovenliness with open doors
A Fata Morgana of infinite meadows which the farmers
Overflew on strong-winged squawking
Tractors undertaking all sorts of
Busywork with diverse trailers
Now black bird towers
Rise in their place the storm blows them
Upwards into low clouds snow covers
The ashcolored earth the corpse
Under withered long moldering skin.

When we run to the door because of
Steps it is always in vain only the keen
Wind the unbroken even
Fine-ground snow lie outside
Black mocking eyes and the darkness.
We are buried here for years
Sit by the snow fire thawing
Our black-frozen souls.
Already the whiteness looks like
A field of lilies we are totally dazed
By all that juniper the fat meat of
Freshly slaughtered pigs in the smoke.

Bewandtnis

Der Pfau verachtet den Hühnerstall lieber
Sitzt er nachts auf dem Schornstein
Wärmt sich den Steiß. Das dünne Mondlicht
Macht ihn gewaltig eine Feder das Auge darauf
Bedeckte mein Fenster. Am Morgen
Fliegt er vom Dach es wird hell.

Thereby Hangs a Tale

The peacock scorns the chicken coop he'd rather
Sit on the chimney at night
Warming his rump. The thin moonshine
Makes him gigantic a feather the eye of it
Covered my window. In the morning
He flies from the roof it is getting light.

Die Geologen

Die abgeschlagene Sonne tagelang
Außerhalb dieser Dampfwelt.
Der Nebel flattert dicht daß den Vöglein
Die Stirnen zerbersten im Flug.
Nach Menschen brauchen wir
Gar nicht zu fragen nirgendwo
Nirgendwer kein Briefbote
Nicht der Hausierer mit
Hexenschußpflastern Fremdlinge
Teilen sich durch Erschüttrungen mit
Die bellende Kartaun Tilly
Oder die Schweden.

Der Sprengmeister und der Bohr-
Meister tappen im Milchwald mit
Brennenden Lunten schlagen hin
Über Stolperwurzeln die heidnischen Gruben
Sammeln sie auf, der grüne Koffer
Dynamit in prallen eckigen Säckchen
Kracht auf den Opfertisch bedenklich
Neigen sich entwurzelt Bäume.
Die Alte prustet ins Fäustchen
Sitzt auf der Gasblase eh und je gibt sie
Für kein Seelenheil her die Erdvermesser
Beißen ins Gras.

The Geologists

The weary sun for days on end
Beyond this steamworld
Fog flutters dense bursting the little
Birds' foreheads in flight
Don't even ask about
People not anywhere
Nobody no mailman
Not the pedlar with plasters
Against lumbago and witchcraft strangers
Make themselves known with shockwaves
The bellowing carthoun Tilly
Or the Swedes.

The blasting master and the bore
Master grope about in the milkwood with
Burning fuses trip
Over stumbleroots the pagan pits
Catch them the green suitcase
Dynamite packed in square little sacks
Cracks on the sacrificial altar uprooted
Trees list precarious
The old one laughs up her sleeve
Sits on the gaspool from ever on
Won't give it up for any salvation the tampering
Measurers bite the dust.

Kahlfrost

Die Natur hat einen Grad der Kargheit
Und Verkommenheit erreicht der durch nichts
Überboten werden kann, grau und verkrustet
Tiefgefroren liegt die Erde darnieder kein Aufwand
Mit jagenden Wolken Schneefall ovalen Sonnen
Die Verzauberungen sind gänzlich abgeschlossen
Die Feste wurden sämtlich gefeiert die erwarteten
Kälber geboren die Fenster im Kuhstall lange geputzt.
Die Bäuerinnen häkeln schwarze verdrossene Spitzen.

Frost

Nature has reached a degree of poverty
And decay that can't be surpassed
Gray and encrusted deep frozen
The earth is lying down no display
Of racing clouds snowfall oval suns
The enchantments are utterly at an end
All the festivals have been observed the expected
Calves were born the windows in the cowshed are clean.
The farmers' wives crochet black peevish lace.

Beständig

Der schwarzbunte Himmel über den
Backsteinhäusern gelben Wiesen
Die sich neigenden blattlosen Bäume
Die rote Katze auf dem Sockel der
Klärgrube das freischwebende Dach
Einer zusammenfallenden Scheune
Verbreiten in Kumpanei mit der
Mittagsstille eine süße Melancholie.
Traumverloren findet die Schere
Sich am Hals zurecht schneidet Haar
In dicken Bündeln singenden Tons
Sanft kehrt sie ins Schubfach zurück
Die Haarschnitterin sieht einen Vogel
Rückwärts fliegen glaubt nicht an Gott.

Steadfast

The black dappled sky above the
Brick houses the yellow fields
Leafless trees bowing down
The red cat on the rim of the
Cesspool the floating roof
Of a crumbling barn are in
Cahoots with the noonday hush
Spreading a sweet wistfulness.
Dreamlike the scissors find their way
About the neck cut hair
On a singing note in thick bundles
Meek they return to the drawer
The haircutter watches a bird fly
Backwards she does not believe in God.

Nördlicher Garten

Die Rotdrosseln stehen im Regen
Der Südwind blies sie mir auf die
Füße das Rot steckt ihnen tief
Unter den matten Flügeln.
Klingelndes Rufen der Herde
Bewirtung eh der Flug wieder beginnt
Nach Kelloselka den Vogelbeeren
Im Garten des wortlosen Dichters.
Wie Rotdrosseln zwischen Blättern
Rascheln Bilder im Kopf, stark
Schlägt das Herz unter dem Flachmann
Wenn er vom Gletscher zu Tal fährt
Rauchender glücklicher Reifen.

Northerly Garden

The thrushes stand in the rain
The south wind has blown them at
My feet the red stuck deep
Under tired wings.
Ringing calls of some herd
Hospitality before the flight begins again
To Kelloselka and the berries of mountain ash
In the wordless poet's garden.
Like redwinged thrushes among leaves
Pictures rustle in the head, the flat-
Lander's heart beats strong
When he races downhill from the glacier
A smoke-trailing happy wheel.

Willkommen

Wenn das Eis reißt der Wind
Umspringt die Richtungen wechselt
Dem Licht eine Gasse schlägt wieder
Zustopft hohen gebogenen Bäumen
Die letzten gezählten Blätter abnimmt
Naht der Metzger hält seinen Hut fest
Und betritt die weißgescheuerte Küche.

Welcome

When the ice rips the wind
Shifts changing directions
Making a breach for the light plugging it
Up again taking away the last counted leaves
Of the high bent trees
The butcher approaches holding on to his hat
And enters the white-scoured kitchen.

Anfang des Tages

Die Treibhausblumen leuchten in der
Dämmrigen Diele, hinterm Rücken des Hauses
Feiert die morgendliche sehr frische Sonne
Märzorgien die Alte ist wohl durch den
Winter gelangt schmückt sich mit Glaube
Liebe Hoffnung die Krone stachelt Vögel
Zu Lärm an sie schleppen Halme stürzen
Und steigen und Katzen schweben nach
Der Maulwurf beginnt sein einsames Handwerk
Alte Frauen gehen in Gärten sie zählen
Blumen vertreiben Hühner glätten Mulden
Sind sehr zufrieden über der Erde wenn sie
Der Männer gedenken die schon am Rande
Des Dorfes angelangt sind in Särgen.

Daybreak

The hothouse flowers glow in the
Dusky hall, behind the back of the house
The very fresh morning sun celebrates
Orgies of March the crone's gotten well through
Winter decks out her crown with Faith
Love and Hope stings birds into
Uproar hauling of stalks they dive
And soar and cats glide after
The mole sets about his lonesome trade
Old women go into gardens count
Flowers chase chickens smooth over hollows
Are very satisfied above the ground when they
Think of the men who've already been
Handed beyond the village in coffins.

Reigen

Die bleichen flechtenbewachsenen Maste
Beginnen zu kreisen am Mittag
Wenn der Wanderer naht die weiße
Lenzsonne über dem Scheitel auf
Schwankendem Boden sein Blut
Schießt durch enge silberne Pfeifen
Das Licht zerspringt in glühenden
Überfließenden Kesseln Kaninchen
Rollen im Torfstich.

Roundelay

The pale lichen-clad masts
Begin to turn round and round at noon
When the wanderer comes near white
April sun upon his crown on
Quaking ground his blood
Shooting through tight silver pipes
The light splits apart overflows
Fiery kettles rabbits
Tumble in cut peat.

Die Wolken

Nun ist die Welt hinter den Scheiben
In stärkerem Maße ein ausgebreiteter
Schwarzgemalter Worpsweder Bogen
Die Moore glänzen es gibt nur noch
Moore der Mensch einer Mutter Sohn geht
Getreten geschlagen ein Bastard hin
An dunkelroten überfließenden Bächen
Der erstarrte Wald birgt die Totenvögel
Zäune halten gepfähltes Leben
O die schwermütigen lackbemalten
Harten die Menschen verwüstenden Wolken
Traumverlorenen Bäume über den
Hündisch geduckten Häusern aus denen
Rauch kriecht unbändiges stumpfes Verlangen
Nach Tanz schäumenden Schützenfesten
Niedergeworfenen weißgekleideten Mädchen
Faustkämpfen wenn das Messer schwer
In den Kleidern liegt und ins Licht will

The Clouds

Now the world behind the panes
Looks even more like a spread
Black-painted Worpswede sheet
The moors shine there is nothing but
Moors man a mother's son
Stepped upon beaten a bastard goes past
Dark-red overflowing streams
The petrified forest shelters deathbirds
Fences hold up life impaled
Oh the mournful lacquer-daubed
Hard man-ravaging clouds
Trees lost in dreams above the
Paltry cowering houses where
Smoke creeps a tremendous dull desire
For dance foaming country fairs
Tumbled white-clad girls
Fistfights when the knife is heavy
In the clothes wants out into light.

Worpswede is a village in the Devil's Moor near Bremen, where Otto
Modersohn and his friend Mackensen founded an artists colony in 1895.

König Philipp

Die Schwalben sind da die
Kartoffeln durchbrechen faltig
Voller Sorgen die Erde
Alle Wiesen begrünten sich festlich
Schwebt Schaumkraut über den Halmen
Die Felder sind rundum bestellt
Letzte Fröste fressen die Kirschen
Wenn alte Weiber den Schlaf
Nicht opfern und Rauch
Aus Teerfässern steigen lassen.
Aber die Drosseln schreien um Phillipp!
Sich die Kehlen wund früh am Morgen.

King Philip

The swallows are here the
Potatoes wrinkled and full of
Care break through the earth
All meadows turned festively green
Cardamine floats above the stalks
The fields are tilled round about
Last frosts bite the cherries
Unless old women give up
Sleep to let smoke
Fly from tar pots.
But the thrushes cry their throats
Sore over Philip! early in the morning.

Zeitung

Spät wurden in diesem Jahr die Schafe geschoren
Die Kühe drängten sich länger als sonst in den Ställen
Wenn die Bauern elektrische Zäune flickten
Hörten sie diesmal umsonst auf den Kuckuck
Die Schwalben kamen im letzten Moment hatten Mühe
Auf leichten Flügeln ihr Mahl zu erlangen.
Dieser harte und gnadenlose sehr lange Winter
Der Schneepflug am heiligen Osterfest ließ die Menschen
Erstarren und unempfindlich gegen geringe Freude
Ihre Sisyphosarbeit tun alle Rosen
Waren auf Jahre erfroren und noch in kleinen Blättern
Fanden sich Mutmaßungen über kommende Kriege.

Tidings

The sheep were shorn late this year
In the stalls the cows jostled each other longer than usual
While the farmers mended electrified fences
They listened in vain for the cuckoo this time
The swallows arrived at the last moment had trouble
Getting their meal on light wings.
This hard and merciless very long winter
The snowplow for Holy Easter made the people
Go numb and do their Sisyphean work
Indifferent to little joys all roses were
Frozen for years to come and even in small leaflets
Conjectures about future wars.

Unauslöschbares Bild

Das müssen die Vorgängerinnen im Blick gehabt haben
im Frühjahr oftmals durch die Jahrhunderte sonst
könnte mein Seelencomputer nicht so zu rasseln begin-
nen Verbindungen knüpfend zu bestimmter Empfin-
dung. Dieses alte einfache Bild ist ein gewaltiger
Anblick, das bewirken die Dolomiten nicht nicht der
Zürichsee in verschiedener schöner Beleuchtung. Ruck-
artige Freude, die Gewißheit auf der Erde zu stehn.
Nie habe ich ehrwürdige Schränke Barockgemälde alte
Ringe geerbt
Nur die Erfahrung steckt in den Knochen
Einer Wiese im fettesten Grün
Gelbe und weiße Blumen und blaue
Glänzende niedrigfliegende die Gräser
Berührende Schwalben in ihren
Schnellen lebendigen Mustern.

Inerasable Image

Often in spring through the centuries
This must have caught an ancestress' eye else
My soul's computer couldn't start clacking so
Knotting connections to definite
Feeling. This old simple picture is a powerful
Sight, not the Dolomites not the Lake of Zurich
In diverse fine illumination effect anything like it.
A jolt of joy, the certainty to stand on earth.
I never inherited worthy old cupboards Baroque
Paintings antique rings
Only experience sticks in the bones
Of a meadow in fattest green
Yellow and white flowers and blue
Gleaming low flying swallows
Touching the grasses in their
Quick lively patterns.

Bewegung

Die Nachbarhäuser zerstreuen sich wieder
Die Fliehkraft der Erde der üppige Frühling
Drängen sie an den Horizont Koppeln und Wiesen
Dehnen sich aus die aufgestellten Kühe
Legen lange Wege zurück die Blumen
Dornen und Vogelnester viel dichtes Gesträuch
Ist nun ins Land geworfen die Eichen
Holen ihr Laub vor schließen mich ein.

Movement

The neighboring houses disperse again
The centrifugal force of earth the opulent spring
Push them to the horizon paddocks and meadows
Expand the assembled cows
Set off on their long way the flowers
Thorns bird-nests much dense shrubbery
Is thrown into the countryside the oaks
Haul out their leaves enclose me.

Gloria

Das Reich der Pflanzen gewinnt an Boden
Breitet sich aus unaufhaltsam und mächtig
Seine Farben die Banner in fünf Etagen
Wehen an Eschenschäften auf in den Himmel
Die platzenden Wiesen verschlingen die Kühe
Hellgrüne Ketten von Erbsen des Rettichs
Durchziehen den Garten kopfgroße Blumen
Locken Hummeln und Käfer ins Licht
Das närrische Unkraut viel Stengel
In eine Pore gestopft rote Pestwurz
Welscher Kümmel Knöterich Mohn alles drängt sich
In alter Weise unter der Sonne die letzten
Patronen des Winters schönes Wasser
Darin nun die Frösche rudern
Und wie verschwenderisch gehen die Veilchen
Mit ihren Kindern um eine Schleppe
Frischer Pflanzen in allen Größen
Führt vom Hügel über die Wege die übrigen
Beete die Treppe unter die Tür

Gloria

The plant kingdom gains ground
Spreads itself out immense and strong
Its colors the banners in five tiers
Flutter on ash tree poles up to the sky
The bursting pastures devour the cows
Bright green chains of radish and peas
Run through the garden flowers the size of a head
Lure beetles and bumblebees into the light
The foolish weeds many stalks
Stuffed in one pore red plaguewort
Welsh cumin knotgrass and poppies everything crowds
Under the sun in the old way
The frogs now paddle in lovely water
Last ammunition of winter
And how spendthrift the violets are
With their children a train of new
Plants in all sizes
Leads from the hill over the paths the other
Beds the stairs under the door.

Die Ausschweifung

Keinen Hut nur die Hennahaare aufm Kopf
Unter Mittag leidenschaftlich den Pfeilen
Der Sonne ausgesetzt in strahlenden Beeten
Ohne Schatten von Haus und Baum
Kniend verwünschtes Unkraut ausreißen
Wunderbare sich selbst verschlingende
Wiedergebärende Kreise lackrote Räder
Drehn sich im Kopf Schwärze und
Schwindel brechende Dämme
Hundegebell am Rand des Bewußtseins
Der Kuckuck aus einer anderen Welt
Die Reihen schlingern im Beet Borretsch
Und Pimpernell tanzt durch die Melde
Nur die Hände sind ganz lebendig
Sinken und steigen
Wie ein Paar Schwalben.

Excess

No hat only the henna hair on the head
Fervent exposure to the noonday sun's
Arrows in radiant beds
Without a shadow of tree or house
Kneeling to pull accursed weeds
Wondrous circles devouring each other
Rebirthing red lacquered wheels
Turn in the head blackness and
Dizziness breaches in dams
Dogs barking on the edge of awareness
The cuckoo from another world
Borage sways in its rows
And pimpernel dances through the pigweed
Only the hands are fully alive
Sink and rise
Like a pair of swallows.

Spieluhr

Der verwunschene verwilderte Garten
Hält das alte sich neigende Haus
Vergißmeinnichtteppiche blaues Email
In zerfallenden Fundamenten
Ich sah die Mauern der Schmiede den Ring
Ackerpferde zu halten
Roßkäfer laufen am Mittag
Über schmale unveränderte Wege
Der zugeschüttete Brunnen rauscht
Ein Vogel singt mit zerbrochener Stimme.

Musical Clock

The spellbound overgrown garden
Holds the old leaning house
Forget-me-not carpets blue enamel
In crumbling foundations
I saw the walls of the forge the ring
That tethered the farmhorses
Clegs fly at noon
Along narrow unchanged paths
The blocked-up spring murmurs
A bird sings with a broken voice.

Die Dämmerung

Es ist dunkelgrün unter dem Regen
Den alten Gewölben der Eichen
Halshoch das ungeschnittene Gras
Die tiefen schleifenden Wolken
Treffen Menschen die auf dem Grund
Des Meeres in versunkenen Dörfern
Träumerisch umgehn und Hunde schweben
Durch ein widersinniges Dasein
Die schwarzen Algen der treibende Tang
Schwimmenden Vögel fliegenden Fische
Bringen viel Unruhe mit sich
Über den Dächern sehn wir die Kiele
Englischer Kriegsschiffe ziehn.

The Dusk

It is dark green under the rain
The ancient vaults of oaks
Neck-high the uncut grass
The deep dragging clouds
Come upon people who go about
Dreamy in foundered villages on
The bottom of the sea and dogs float
Through an absurd existence
The black seaweed the drifting kelp
Swimming birds flying fish
Bring along much unrest
Above the roofs we see the keels of
English battleships move.

Gärtners Weltbild

Die Erde ist flach ein Teller
Die Sonne wandert von Ost nach West
Winde fallen aus ihrer Richtung
Kälte bringen sie Dürre und makellos
Tiefgrüne Felder langwierige Plagen
Goldgebänderter Raupen ein Riese
Liegt der Garten im Garten
Das Rückgrat die Rippen die Wege
Wasseradern verzweigt unterm Pelz
Die wetterwendische Haut
Des Gärtners gleicht schon der Erde
Schöne Falten und Augenmuster Geduld
Und Hoffnung mit Löffeln gefressen platte
Landgängerfüße vom Gießkannentragen
Die leichte ausdauernde Seele
Geht und kommt wie sie will.

Gardener's World-View

The earth is flat a plate
The sun travels from east to west
Winds change their course
Bring cold drought and impeccably
Deep green fields lingering plagues
Of gold-striped caterpillars a giant
The garden lies in the garden
The backbone the ribs the paths
Water-veins branching under the fur
The gardener's weatherset skin
Already resembles the earth
Fine furrows and eye designs patience
And hope consumed by the spoonful a flat-footed
Walk from lugged watering-cans
The light steadfast soul
Comes and goes as it wills.

Die Entrückung

Die Sonne schleudert unbarmherzige Hitze
Dem Grabenden auf den gebeugten Rücken
Flüche hört er verschollner Gestalten
Den uralten Kuckuck und das Gewese
Der frommen einfältigen Lerchen er sieht
Im weißen brechenden Licht
Wolkenlos Gottes Thron, auf den Stufen
Die heiligen Ackerpferde stehn
Die nun allerorts fehlen.

The Rapture

The sun hurls unmerciful heat
Onto the bent digger's back
He hears the curses of lost beings
The ancient cuckoo and the airs
Of the gentle artless larks he sees
In the white refracting light
Unclouded God's throne, on the steps
The holy plow-horses that
Now are everywhere missing.

Steinherz

Kalte Füße mitten im Sommer nach der
Pfingsthitze der Backofenglut endloser Tage
Schafskälte sie geht den geschorenen
Tieren den Menschen hin auf die Haut
Macht ein tragbares unempfindlich
Schönrauhes Herz das die Bilder
Verschiedener junger Kriege
Auf dem Planeten aushalten läßt.

Nach der Nacht im Wirtshaus gehen die Bauern
Reumütig Steckrüben pflanzen im Wind.
Die Bäume verneigen sich und es blüht
Mit blanken Tellern verwunschner Hollunder
Totenaugen im Schatten der Blätter
Selbstvergessenes Plappern und Seufzen
Runde dörfliche Regen
Schütten sich aus und die Vögel
Rufen Menschennamen über die Felder.

Stoneheart

Cold feet in the middle of summer after
Hot Whitsuntide the bake-oven heat of endless days
Goosebump chills get to the shorn
Animals' the people's skin
Produce a bearable resistant
Rugged heart that can endure
The visions of assorted young
Wars on the planet.

After the night in the pub the farmers go
Penitent in the wind planting turnips.
The trees bow and the spellbound
Elder-bush blooms with blank plates
Eyes of the dead in the shadow of leaves
Self-forgetful chatter and sighs
Round rustic rains
Pour themselves out and the birds
Cry human names over the fields.

Augentrost

Das grüne Gewebe des Gartens wiederkehrende
Muster aus Zwiebelschäften rankenden Erbsen
Fremde Entwürfe die Kürbisblätter Licht
Und Schatten in aufgebundnen Tomaten zärtliche
Kugeln Kohl und Salat Petersilienkanten
Treuer Schachtelhalm Woche für Woche
Geneigtes dunkles Kartoffelkraut über den
Furchen und Akeleien fliegen am Wegrand.

Eyebright

The garden's green fabric recurring
Patterns of onion stalks climbing peas
The strange designs of pumpkin leaves light
And shadow in staked tomatoes tender
Globes cabbage and lettuce parsley borders
Faithful horse-tail week after week
Prone dark potato tops over the
Furrows and columbines fly along the way.

Kleine Vergangenheit

Die Köpfe der mannshohen Spiräen
Sahen ins Fenster und leuchteten
In der kurzen Dunkelheit Ende Juni.
Hollunderlichter schwankten am Zaun
Die Schattenrisse der Hufeisennasen
Standen vorm ausgeblichenen Himmel.

Past Perfect

The heads of hollyhocks tall as a man
Looked in at the window and glowed
In the brief darkness end of June.
Elder lights wavered by the fence
The silhouettes of horseshoe noses
Stood out against the bleached sky.

Musikstunde

Seine Mutter lehrt meine Gartenfinger
Über die Tasten zu springen
Das Pianoforte hat einen Riß
Bellt daß dem Sahnekännchen
Widerstandslos der Henkel abbricht.

Ich wende mich sanften Dingen zu
Wie der Hausherr im Rollstuhl
Die Gartentreppe hinabfährt
Über die grauen Schleifenblumen
Und keine Spur hinterläßt.

Music Lesson

His mother teaches my garden fingers
To leap across the keys
The pianoforte has a crack
Barks and the creampot's
Handle unresisting breaks off.

I turn towards mellow things
As the master of the house
Rides down the garden stairs in
The wheelchair over gray candytuft
Leaving no trail.

Raben

Die Bäume in diesen windzerblasenen
Das Land überrollenden Himmeln
Sind höher als die zusammengeduckten
Gluckenähnlichen Kirchen, und Wolken
Durchfliegen die Kronen die Vögel
Steigen von Ast zu Ast kohlschwarze Raben
Flattern den heidnischen Göttern
Hin auf die Schultern und krächzen
Den Alten die Ohren voll alle Sterblichen
Werden verpfiffen schlappe Seelen
Über den Wurzeln und ohne Flügel.

Ravens

In these windblown skies
Rolling across the land the trees
Are higher than the churches
That crouch like broody hens and clouds
Fly through their crowns the birds
Climb from branch to branch coal-black ravens
Flutter to the pagan gods'
Shoulders and croak in
Their old ears squealing on all
Mortals slack souls
Over the roots and without wings.

Wetterbaum

Die grasende hinkende Taube
Blickt fromm wenn verschimmelte Körner
Aus der Greisenhand regnen.
Über dem roten zerfallenden Haus
Die Schwelle längst eingenommen
Von Schöllkraut und Kletten
Über zersplitterten Blätterkronen
Erhebt sich ein firnweißer Baum.
Der aufgeblähte Schweinekadaver
Das Grausen am Wegrand
Versinkt in Gewitterblumen.

Weathertree

The grazing limping pigeon
Looks meek when moldy kernels
Rain from the old man's hand.
Over the red crumbling house
The doorstep long since seized
By swallowwort and burs
Over splintered leafy crowns
Rises a snow-white tree.
The bloated carcass of a pig
Dread by the roadside
Sinks into thunderstorm flowers.

Lamento

Alles wächst mir über den Kopf
Kletterrosen angenommene Bäume
Lange vergessen die knorrigen Pfähle
Boreas standzuhalten die sanften
Wassergüsse und Torf und Reisig
Über die wunden Füße vor Wochen
Kämmte ich ihnen Kerfe und Raupen
Körbeweis aus jetzt stehn sie
Grün und elegant an den Ecken
Lungern ums Haus sehen auf mich
Ihren Sklaven rauschend herab
Und werden mich glatt überleben
Bohnen pflücke ich von der Leiter
Der Kürbis flegelt sich faul in den
Beeten Sonnenblumen und Mais
Klopfen mir auf die Schultern
Das Kind geht in meinen Schuhn
Erhaben über den Wolken.

Lamentation

Everything grows over my head
Climbing roses adopted trees
Those long forgotten knobby sticks to
Resist Boreas a gentle watering
Peat and brushwood on
The wounded feet weeks ago
I combed out their insects and grubs
By the basket now they stand
Splendid and green at the corners
Lounge about the house look rustling
Down upon me their slave
And will clean outlive me
I pick beans from the ladder
The lazy pumpkin lolls in its
Bed sunflowers and corn
Slap me on the back
The child walks in my shoes
Sublime above the clouds.

Atempause

Der Himmel ist rauchgrau aschgrau mausgrau
Bleifarben steingrau im Land
Des Platzregens der Dauergewitter
Die aufgequollenen Wiesen die Gärten
Verfaulen und Hunden sind über Nacht
Flossen gewachsen sie tauchen
Nach jedem silbernen Löffel der
Aus dem Fenster fällt wenn augenblicklich
Behäbige Marmeladen bereitet werden
In Küchen bei gutem Wetter durchflogen
Von Bäurinnen Heu im Gewand Dampf
Im Hintern auf Rübenhacken am Mittag.

Breather

The sky is smokegray ashgray mousegray
Leadcolored stonegray in the land
Of cloudbursts of continuous rain
The swollen meadows the gardens
Decay and dogs have grown
Flippers over night they dive
After every silver spoon that
Falls from the window at this moment when
Complacent jams are made
In kitchens the farmers' wives
Fly through in fine weather
Hay in their clothes steam
In their behinds to hoe turnips at noon.

Leben

Der Wind öffnet und schließt
Unaufhörlich die Stalltür
Winseln und Stöhnen
Rings in den Lüften
Wellen durchlaufen den Körper
Eines fuchsroten Katers der über
Die ungeschnittenen Wiesen geht.

Life

Unceasing the wind shuts and
Opens the barn door
Whimpers and groans
Round about in the air
Ripples run through the body
Of a fox-red tom-cat
Moving through uncut meadows.

Müdigkeit

Die stille Nachbarin hinter der Hecke
Fieberrosen im Angesicht
Niederfallender Blumen
Sanftes Uhrengeräusch
O die vergeblichen Wünsche die
Wiederkehrenden Blumen.

Tiredness

The quiet neighbor behind the hedge
Fever roses in her face
The soft clocksound of
Dropping blossoms
Oh the fruitless wishes the
Reappearing flowers.

Zugeflogene Rose

Ersprießlicher ist der Umgang mit Pflanzen
Sie kehren wieder oder es herrscht
Gewißheit daß sie in einem einzigen Sommer
Ihr grünes Leben verschleudern Unfälle
Sind leicht zu ertragen die abgemähte
Einst zugeflogene Rose
Wird durch den Kürbis ersetzt und die
Bäume sind fast unschlagbar
Dauerhafter als der eigene Leib
Braucht der Liebhaber sich nicht
Um ihr Fortkommen sorgen der Tod
Hinsinkender sturmgebrochener Riesen
Ist ein erhabener schmerzloser Anblick.

Tossed Rose

More profitable is an acquaintance with plants
They return or else it is
Certain that they will waste
Their green life in a single summer accidents
Are easy to bear the mowed down
Once caught rose
Is replaced by the pumpkin and the
Trees are almost unsurpassed
More durable than one's own body
No lover needs worry
About their departure the death of
Falling stormbroken giants
Is an exalted painless sight.

Der Morgen

Zephir haucht Kühlung über die Wiesen
Trägt den Geruch frischen Brots
Liederlich mit sich am Anfang
Sonnenverbrannter glühender Tage
Ich geh meiner Wege Floras Geschöpfe
Ordergemäß mit Wasser versehn allerhand Finken
Treiben mich an leichtbewegliche
Kehlen bis Kälber den Grasplatz erreichen
Gähnende Bauern Federn im Haar
Ihre Mähmaschinen besteigen mit Hü und Hott
Wie im Traum in die Gemarkungen fahren.

The Morning

Zephyr breathes coolness across the meadows
Carries the fragrance of fresh bread
Slovenly with it at the start of
Sunburned incandescent days
I go my ways furnish Flora's creatures
With water according to orders all kinds of finches
Urge me on nimble
Throats until the calves come to the pasture
Yawning farmers feathers in their hair
Mount mowing machines with gee up and whoa
Drive to the fields as if in a dream.

Weglos

Die Wege im Garten sind untergegangen
Alle Pflanzen verstrickt und verknotet
Ein lebendiger schreiender Teppich.
Das Volk geneigter Sonnenblumen
Hat eine Mauer errichtet.
Es bleibt nichts andres als schwebend
Der Nabel die Zehen deuten zu Boden
Den Rock aufgebunden über dem
Sitzfleisch das im Sommer nichts taugt
Der Arbeit nachkommen in leichter
Überirdischer Haltung rauchend die
Bienenpfeife.

Trackless

The paths in the garden are buried
All plants entwined and knotted
A living carpet.
The slanting crowd of sunflowers
Has erected a wall.
Nothing remains but going to work
Suspended in air navel and toes
Turned to the ground the skirt
Tied up over the seat that's no good
For summer smoking
The bee pipe in an easy celestial
Pose.

Die Stille

Mittags spielt das Klavier von allein
Die Mahlerschen Posthornkonzerte
Angehaltener Abschied herzzerreißend
In knisternden Blumen.
Im anderen Laub
Schwarze Trübsal Geräusch
Sich berührender Blätter.

The Stillness

At noon the piano plays Mahler's
Posthorn Concerts by itself
Sustained farewells heart-rending
Among rustling flowers.
In other foliage
Black grief the sound of
Leaves touching.

Blaue Kugel

Wenn ich mir jetzt einen Pfarrherrn
Meines Vaters Vater betrachte
Wie er vor Jahren den Garten betrat
Die Sonne schoß durch die Zweige
Die Ranken Jelängerjelieber
Streiften sein Predigermaul
Er sah in der kopfgroßen gläsernen
Kugel die gebogene Welt
Zuvörderst sich selbst im glänzenden
Schwarz einen alten Hut
Auch aufm Kopf wie er atmete wie die
Derbe polnische Landluft
In ihn strömte der Nase entwich
Er blies einen Falter
Nach Krotoszyn hin und die Sonne
Wärmte den Leib ihm gehörte
Der Tag hier er ging
Ohne an jemand zu denken
In die runden gewölbten Wälder
Es ist ein merkwürdiges Gefühl
Ihn so aufrecht zu sehen in seiner
Gegenwärtigen Zeit die auch in Zukunft
Vergangenheit heißt wie die meine.

Blue Garden Ball

When I now consider a parson
My father's father how
Years ago he stepped into the garden
The sun was shooting through the branches
The tendrils of honeysuckle
Brushed his preacher's mouth
He saw in the headsized glass
Ball the bent world
First and foremost himself in shiny
Black an old hat
On his head how he breathed how the
Coarse Polish country air
Streamed into him escaped his nose
He blew a butterfly
Towards Krotoszyn and the sun
Warmed his body to him here
Belonged the day he went
Without thinking of anyone
Into the round vaulted woods
It is a strange feeling
To see him so upright in his
Time which in future too
Will be called past like mine.

Katzenleben

Aber die Dichter lieben die Katzen
Die nicht kontrollierbaren sanften
Freien die den Novemberregen
Auf seidenen Sesseln oder in Lumpen
Verschlafen verträumen stumm
Antwort geben sich schütteln und
Weiterleben hinter dem Jägerzaun
Wenn die besessenen Nachbarn
Immer noch Autonummern notieren
Der Überwachte in seinen vier Wänden
Längst die Grenzen hinter sich Ließ.

Catlives

But the poets love cats
The uncontrollable gentle
Free who laze away Novemberrain
On silken seats or in rags
Sleeping dreaming and mute
Give their answer shake themselves and
Live on behind the huntsmen's fence
While zealous neighbors
Keep their eyes on license plates
The watched one inside his four walls
Long ago left the borders behind.

Die Verdammung

Weil ihm zu sterben verwehrt war
Angekettet dem heimischen Felsen der Blick
Auf die ziehenden Wolken gerichtet und immer
Allein die Bilder im Kopf stimmlos
Vom Rufen Anrufen Verdammen
Das Leben fristen war nicht zu bedenken
Göttliche Hinterlist nährte ihn so gewöhnte
Er sich langsam ins Schicksal nach Jahren
Sah er den Adler gern wenn er nahte und sprach
Stotternd mit ihm bei der Verrichtung

Oder mit entzündeten Augen verrenktem Hals
Weil der Flügelschlag ausblieb die niederen Wälder
Aufschub ihm angedeihn ließen um Tage
Harrte er des einzigen Wesens und glaubte
In der Leere des Winds der glühenden Sonne
Wenn der Fittiche Dunkel fürn Augenblick
Erquickung schenkte geborgen zu sein
Liebte den Folterer dichtete Tugend ihm an

Als die Ketten zerfielen der Gott
Müde geworden an ihn noch zu denken
Der Adler weiterhin flog weil kein
Auftrag ihn innezuhalten erreichte
Gelang es ihm nicht sich erheben den
Furchtbaren Ort für immer verlassen
In alle Ewigkeit hält er am Mittag
Ausschau nach seinem Beschatter.

Damnation

Because he was not permitted to die
Chained to the native rock his gaze
Turned towards the moving clouds and always
Alone the pictures in the head voiceless
From calling invoking and cursing
No need to reflect on keeping alive
Divine trickery fed him in time
He got used to his fate years after
Was pleased when the eagle appeared and stuttering
Spoke with him during the rite

Or he awaited with burning eyes craning his neck
When the beat of wings failed the low woods
Granting him delay
Awaited the only being and in the emptiness
Of wind of white-hot sun
When the pinions' darkness for a moment
Gave refreshment believed himself sheltered
Loved the torturer imputed virtue to him

As the chains fell apart the god
Had tired still to think of him
The eagle continued his flights since no
Orders to cease were received
He could not raise himself up
Leave the fearful place for ever
To all eternity keeps looking out at noon
For his overshadower.

Die Flucht

Hans Wurst springt über die Felsen
Der Faltengebirge von Klinge zu Klinge
Sanft ziehen die Flüsse in ihre Meere
Aus den Kesseln der Städte steigt Rauch
Die Friedensstifter in kleinen Privatflugzeugen
Sind pausenlos unterwegs in den Lüften.

The Flight

Merry Andrew jumps over the rocks
Of the folded mountains from blade to blade
Softly the rivers pass into their seas
From the cauldrons of cities rises smoke
The peacemakers in their small private planes
Are always on the move up in the air.

August

Badewannen verschiedenen Stils
Stehn auf den Weiden das bunte Vieh
Brüllt unterm Hundsstern die letzten
Lebenden Blumen leuchten wenn nachts
Der Bauer seine Felder abmäht.

August

Bathtubs of differing styles
Sit in the pastures the colorful livestock
Low under the dogstar the last
Living flowers glow when the farmer
Cuts his fields in the night.

Regenzeit

In den Häusern brennt Licht grüne Äpfel
Leuchten aus abgestorbenen Blättern
Die verdammte Hellhörigkeit heißer Tage
Jedes Wort aus den Kammern Flüche und
Kälbergebrüll explodierende Trecker
Ist dauerndem Rauschen gewichen, lautlos
Wird das Korn auf die Speicher geblasen.

Rainy Season

Lights are on in the houses green apples
Glow between withered leaves
The hot days' damned keenness of hearing
Every word from the bedrooms curses and
Lowing calves exploding tractors
Has given way to constant rustling, soundless
Is the grain blown into the granaries.

Die Erinnerung

Eine dreibeinige schwangere Katze
Humpelt über den Weg
Und Elstern chinesische Seidenpapiere
Spreizen sich in der Luft
Wenn ich Milch in die Kannen schöpfe
Seh ich durchs Spinnengitter
Der Urahn auf sonniger Heide schnitt
Kraut für das Schaf Gras für die Ziege.
In den Taschen nur Donnerkeile
Dachte er angesichts dieser Armut
Das Land erreichen hinter den Wassern.
Das Dreibein die Vögel durchkreuzen den Blick.
Ich gehe im Regen über die Wiesen.

Remembrance

A three-legged expectant cat
Limps across the road
And magpies Chinese silk papers
Spread themselves wide in the air
While I ladle milk into jugs
I see through the spider lattice
The ancestor on the sunny heath cutting
Weeds for the sheep grass for the goats
In his pocket only thunderstones
He thought in the face of his poverty
To reach the land behind the waters.
The three-leg the birds cross the view.
I walk in the rain over meadows.

Gebannt

Tagelanges Rauschen des Winds
In alten bewegten Bäumen
Er fährt ihnen ins harte Laub
Daß die ausgebreiteten Äste
Aufgeworfen werden mit flehender
Widersetzlicher Gebärde
Schon fallen Eicheln zu Boden
Hellgrüne Pfeifchen voll Bitternis
Das junge erstaunte Vieh
Duckt sich über den Wurzeln ins Gras
Anhaltendes hohes Tönen die singenden
Zungen die Blätter der Nachhall
Hinter der Stirn erzeugt eine Demut
Die reglos gefangen hält.

Spellbound

Daylong rustling of the wind
In old moved trees
He drives into their hard leaves
That the spread branches
Fling up in a pleading and
Rebellious gesture
Already acorns fall to earth
Light green little pipes full of bitterness
The young surprised cattle crouch
In the grass near the roots
Sustained high tones the singing
Tongues the leaves the resonance
Behind the forehead bring forth a humility
That holds transfixed and captive.

Albumblatt

Die schwarzweißen wiederkäuenden Kühe
Liegen zärtliche Klumpen auf
Erzengelwurzwiesen die Katze
Gleicher Farben duckt sich am Zaun
Drauf Elstern springen und schrein
Unter tiefhängendem feuchten Gewölk
Geht die zugeknöpfte Bäuerin im Joch
Erfüllbarer Pflichten schnellen Schritts
Lackierte Kohlköpfe schneiden
Begleitet von Schmetterlingen.

Album Leaf

Black and white cows chewing the cud
Lie tender lumps in the
Archangels' aromatic meadows a cat
Of similar colors is crouched by the fence
Where magpies leap and cry
Under the low damp clouds
The buttoned-up farmer's wife goes
With a quick step in the yoke of fulfillable duties
To cut lacquered cabbage heads
Attended by butterflies.

Spinnengarn

Nebel weht Töchter des Herbstes
Auf großen blassen Füßen springen sie lautlos
Von Tür zu Tür strecken sich in die Kronen
Der Bäume die nun allerorts Früchte tragen
Heften die Tücher das Laken der Windsbraut
An Dachrinnen fest daß uns der Blick
Verwehrt ist Aussicht ins grüne Land
Durch die Erinnerung geschieht
Einmal der Landkartenleib einer tragenden Kuh
Auftaucht aus feuchtem flatternden Leinen.
Die nahen Blumen der Türsteherwacholder
Sind völlig verstrickt Spinnengarn weißgraue Schnüre
Hängende Brücken verspannte Pfeiler Gewölbe
Um schwarze Beeren und Wassertropfen stumpf
Ohne die abgeschlagene blitzende Sonne.
Nicht der geringste Ruf keine mächtige Stimme
Dringt uns ins Ohr wenn wir frierend
Auf Steintreppen stehn die nirgendhin führen.

Spider's Yarn

Fog wafts daughters of autumn
On large pale feet they leap from door
To door without sound and stretch into the crowns
Of trees that now bear fruit on every side
Fasten the shawls the sheet of the whirlwind's bride
To eaves blocking our view
So that we must see the countryside
Through memory's eye once
The contour map of a cow in calf
Appears in the damp and flapping linen
Nearby flowers the juniper guarding the door
Are all tangled up spider's yarn white gray strings
Suspended bridges strutted piers vaults
Around black berries drops of water dull
Without the stricken sparkling sun
Not the slightest call no mighty voice
Reaches us when we stand freezing
On stone stairs that lead nowhere.

Querfeldein

Wir sprachen unterirdisch erst durch die
Heide Steingräber heulten im Wind dann
Mecklenburg Brandenburg durch und es war
Ein herrlicher Morgen Veilchenwolken
Über Chausseen hochfliegende Schwalben
Wir hörten die Kühe über den Kabeln
Unsere unvergeßlichen treuen Stimmen die
Kiebitze ordentlich schrein die Sicherheit
War mit von der Partie Elke sagte
Wie mühsam es ist Tag und Nacht
Ein Atemloch offen zu halten ich sah sie
Im lichtlosen Wald als es grenzenlos schneite
In durchgelaufenen Turnschuhen stehn.

Cross Country

We talked underground first through the
Heath stone mounds howled in the wind then
Through Mecklenburg Brandenburg and it was
A glorious morning violet-clouds
Over the roads and high-flying swallows
We heard the cows above the cables
Our unforgotten faithful voices the
Pewits really screaming Security
Was in on the thing Elke said
How hard it is day and night to
Keep open a breathing space I saw her stand
In the lightless woods where the snowfall knew no
Bounds her gymshoes worn into holes.

Herbstrauch

Auf den gesegneten Feldern durch
Steckrüben Mais rücken Kolonnen
Pausenlos vor, das panische Vieh
Galoppiert in elektrische Zäune.
Fallschirmspringer über dem Kirchdach
Die eigene ruhmlose Anwesenheit
Im Totenspiel ungewisser Bedeutung
Zerstört den Bewohnern die Sinne
Schüttere Wesen bergen sich
Im Dorf der zermahlenen Steine.

Autumn Smoke

In the blessed fields through
Turnips and corn columns advance
Without pause, the panicked cattle
Gallop into electrified fences.
Their inglorious presence
At the death game of uncertain meaning
Wrecks the inhabitants' wits
Shaken creatures burrow down
In the village of ground stone.

Bäume

Früher sollen sie
Wälder gebildet haben und Vögel
Auch Libellen genannt kleine
Huhnähnliche Wesen die zu
Singen vermochten schauten herab.

Trees

It is reputed that
In former times they formed forests and birds
Also called dragonflies small
Gallinaceous creatures capable of
Song looked down from them.

Weltrand

Die abgeschlagenen Köpfe der Kühe
Schweben im Nebel über den Wiesen
Wenn der gehörnte Pfarrer am Abend
Mit roten Augen im Torfstich umherirrt.
Die letzten Vögel des Sommers reden
Mit vernünftigen menschlichen Stimmen
Es gilt Abschied zu nehmen von allen
Vertrauten Blumen und Blättern.
Halb steht die Sonne über dem
Wald halb ist sie unter.

Edge of the World

The chopped off heads of cows
Float in the fog over the meadows
When the red-eyed cuckold parson
Roams about the peat-bog at evening.
With human voices the last birds
Of summer talk sense
Now it is time to bid farewell to all
Familiar flowers and leaves.
The sun stands half above the
Woods half it is under.

Geröll

Mühlsteine Schleifsteine aufgerissene
Schern spitze Messer wohin ich auch
Blicke leere Himmel abgestorbene
Felder die überschlagenden
Glocken im Turm der Leichenzug
Weitsichtbar auf dem einzigen Hügel
Grabsteine Flursteine der hohe Mut
Flog mit den Schwalben davon.

Rubble

Millstones grindstones wide open
Scissors pointed knives wherever I
Look empty skies withered
Pastures the ringing cracking
Bells in the tower the funeral procession
On the only hill evident from afar
Gravestones fieldstones high hope and courage
Flown off with the swallows.

Unausweichliche Kälte

Ich saß mit einer weißgrauen Katze
Die keinem gehört in der späten
Langsam verlöschenden Sonne
Trägheit umgab uns daß wir
Nicht fähig waren den Ort zu verlassen.
Die Kühe rupften am spärlichen Gras
Und husteten mit menschlicher Stimme
Die Katze war schwanger ein hartes Leben
Zeichnet sich ab vor fallenden Blättern.

Inescapable Cold

I sat in the late slowly fading
Sun with a white and gray cat
That belonged to no one
Dullness ensnared us we could not
Move from the spot.
The cows plucked sparse grass
And coughed with a human sound
The cat was pregnant a hard life
Etched against falling leaves.

Sanfte Jagd

Die lebendigen glühenden Blumen
Taubenblaues Gefieder halshoher Astern
Seeigel-Dahlien gesträubt auf dem Grund
Versunkener Dörfer brennende Liebe
Bevor der Frost sie in einer Nacht
Schwärzt und die Hinrichtung vornimmt
Bringen das Herz unterm Wolfspelz zur Strecke.

Gentle Hunt

The living glowing flowers
Dove-blue plumage of neck high asters
Sea-urchin dahlias in the depths
Of a drowned village this burning love
Before the frost blackens them in one
Night and puts them to death
Bring down the heart under the wolfskin.

Feuerofen

Die Toten steigen im Herbst auf aus den
Strömen und Flüssen willfährige Winde
Führen am Himmel bewegte Bilder den Ausgang
Mördrischer Schlachten vor hingeworfene
Leichen erfrorene Seelen geschnürte
Kehlen Körper von grauen Fetzen gehalten
Schweben über den weggebückten ackernden Menschen
Eh sie zerblasen werden die Sonne
Im Spiegel des Himmels erneut
Trostlos pathetische Wolken
Aufstehn und wandern läßt.

Fiery Oven

In autumn the dead ascend from the
Rivers and streams compliant winds
Present moving pictures in the sky the
Outcome of murderous battles flung
Down corpses frozen souls strangled
Throats bodies held in gray rags
Float above the bentaway workers in the field
Before they are blown apart the sun
In the mirror of heaven once more
Lets desolate solemn clouds
Rise up and wander.

Glashaus

Zäune verlassener Koppeln
Drosseln und Ammern
Ruhlose Seelen fahrendes Volk
Das mich aus Perlenaugen betrachtet
Wenn ich sorglos ohne Bedenken
Über Schwellen steige so süße
Worte im Kopf Bilder vor Augen
Daß noch der Spiegel beschlägt
Herzklopfen schöne
Nelkenbuketts auf den Brüsten der Mund
Vom Allerweltswort dünngeschliffen
Empfindlich wien gläserner Nachttopf
Schönglatt schönrot schaukelnd und
Zweifelnd das Haar.

Glasshouse

Fences of abandoned paddocks
Thrushes and buntings
Restless souls vagrants
Regarding me beady-eyed
When I climb carefree without a thought
Over the pales such sweet
Words in the head pictures before the eyes
Even the mirror steams up
Heartbeatings lovely
Carnation bouquets on the breasts the mouth
Polished thin by smart aleck words
Sensitive like a glass chamber-pot
Fine smooth fine red tossing and
Doubting the hair.

Dunkelheit

Und wenn sich die Stimmen Schwester es
Brennt der Wildgänse nachts überschneiden
Geh ich von Fenster zu Fenster höre die
Sturmgeschüttelten Bäume
Anklopfen um abgefallene Blätter.

Darkness

And when the cries *Sister a*
Fire of the wild geese cross in the night
I go from window to window hear the
Stormshaken trees
Knock at my door for cast off leaves.